Living Out of Darkness

A Personal Journey of Embracing the Bipolar Opportunity

George Denslow

authorHOUSE®

AuthorHouse™
1663 Liberty Drive, Suite 200
Bloomington, IN 47403
www.authorhouse.com
Phone: 1-800-839-8640

© 2009 George Denslow. All rights reserved.

No part of this book may be reproduced, stored in a retrieval system, or transmitted by any means without the written permission of the author.

First published by AuthorHouse 2/27/2009

ISBN: 978-1-4389-0870-0 (sc)

Library of Congress Control Number: 2009901158

Printed in the United States of America
Bloomington, Indiana

This book is printed on acid-free paper.

Dedication

Silence is the beginning and end of all truth.

Before we begin this journey together, I would like to invite spirit to be with us by sharing a moment of silence together.

* * * * * *

Thank you.

I dedicate this book to the healing of my family of origin; may we all continue to find a peace on this journey.

Contents

Prologue	xi
Part One	**1**
What Is Bipolar?	1
Introduction	3
Definitions and Theory	4
What Is Bipolar?	4
A Different Definition	5
Intro to Theory	6
Helicopters	7
Part Two	**9**
A Holistic Approach	9
Introduction	11
Body	11
Drugs and Alcohol	11
Food	15
Exercise	18
Is It Open for Hugs?	22
Massage	23
Snuggle Buddies	24
Mind	26
Intro to Counseling	26
Always Have an Exit Plan	29
Abuse	30
Journaling	31
Now	32
Past	33
Future	34
Daily	34
After-action Reports	35

This, Too, Shall Pass	36
Books A Way Out	37
Music Brainwash Anyone?	42
Workshops	45
Head Banging to Mozart by the River	46
Meditation	48
Energy, Rhythm, Vision	50

Spirit	54
Introduction	54
Help!	56
Daily	57
Gratitude	59

Breathe on the Inside	60
Finding Gratitude in Bipolar	63
Rat Race	63

Part Three	65
A Guided Tour (Up, Down, and Back to Normal)	65
Introduction	67
Going Up	67
Homicidal	67
Super Brain	70
Decision Time	71
The Inside of Huh?	73
Houston, We Have a Probl -click	74
Happy Highs	77

Going Down	77
Empathy Cycle	77
Suddenly	77
Gradually	79
I Felt So Much Better Once I Gave up Hope …81	
Make Love to Your Depression	83

Suicide or Phoenix Rising?	85
"Normal"	88
The Gentle Life	90
An Aborted Launch	91
Part Four	95
The Symbiotic Opportunity	95
An Opportunity as Individuals	96
How We Can Help An Opportunity for Others	99
Hope A Future	100
Epilogue	105

Disclaimer
This book and the information contained in it are intended for the holistic approach of working with bipolar. It is not intended as a replacement for professional help or medication. I am not, nor do I aspire to be, a medical doctor or psychologist in any way, and I recommend that the reader first consult with professionals before trying any of the ideas presented here. This book can be used in conjunction with, not as a replacement for, any ongoing therapies or medication. This book is not about bipolar and relationships; I'm still waiting to read that one myself. This book is about becoming functional as an individual.

Bullshit Indicator Light (BIL)
Oops! I almost forgot: if your BIL goes off at any point, please feel free to acknowledge it. This book is based on personal experience and theory; it is not intended as a replacement or cure for any existing or future treatment of the bipolar disorder. If something you read doesn't ring true for you or your experiences, please honor yourself and disregard it, or think about it and come back to it later.

I come from a long line of bullshit artists. My first children's stories were made up on the spot by my grandfather as I sat on his knee and snuggled up against his chest. He always considered the words as mere suggestions and the pictures were what really counted. I remember my mom would always be laughing, and I learned later on that he would always cater the current story he was telling us to the adults in the room. Some of my stories are composites of numerous experiences. The heart and soul behind this book is about empathy and healing for the bipolar experience.

Prologue

A campfire, long ago … a way it could be again …

It's a clear night the stars are out, sparks drift up from the spruce wood flames. A dark ring is forming around the base of the fire as the snow melts. We are bundled up in bearskins; our tummies are full because the hunters were skillful today. An old woman comes to the fire; it's immediately silent and still. A quiet shiver winds its way up everyone's spine, no one is immune to her immense, silent power. She is our guide in the unknown. She knows the ways of healing. I'm a little child near her feet, scared because I know tomorrow my training with her starts. I don't know why, but the elders have chosen me to be a healer and not a hunter. I don't like hunting anyway, but the healer seems crazy to me. But people think I'm crazy too.
I watch her grey hair sway as she finds a way to her seat by the fire. No one says a word until she grunts, indicating tonight is not a night for words from her. The hunters pick up their tale again from the day's adventures, and I hold my mom tight, because tomorrow I go far away to the caves with the other special children, led by the crazy woman …

There was a time …

There was a time when darkness ruled my life. Internal hell was my mode, continually reinventing insanity around me so that I could retreat further into my shelter space, deep inside. I was a master of the art form of being invisible and miserable in a crowd full of happy people. I was in constant motion throughout my day with jobs, people, friends, and living spaces. I had become the darkness learned long ago, and I perpetuated beliefs around me to avoid the pain of dealing with it. It was a prison. I was aware of the prison I was in and could see the claw marks on my inner walls craving to get out, jumping up to grab the bars and briefly smile at people before my strength to be happy gave out. I would collapse onto the cold stone floor of my cell, surrendering again to the darkness, comforting myself with thoughts of suicide.

Our journey begins …

Part One
What Is Bipolar?

Introduction
When I was seventeen, I had the opportunity to be locked up in a mental institution against my will for being actively suicidal and refusing treatment. I was diagnosed with being bipolar, manic depressive. They wanted to put me on lithium, but they never did. My family doctor and father agreed that I was heavily into how the mind affected the body, and they decided not to force the issue of medications.

I was released five weeks later on my own recognizance, to begin my life's journey as an adult. I had one purpose in life: not to lose my freedom again, ever. I believed that God doesn't make junk and that I was created this way for a reason. My mission in life became to find a way to live without medications.

By hook or by crook and, at times, by sheer guts, I've discovered a way and a why. This book is the result of twenty years of actively developing and living a holistic, spiritual approach to thriving with bipolar, using my body and my life, as a guinea pig.

This is not a traditional book or a conventional approach to mental health. If you have a mental "opportunity" and have been directed to or have found this book, I'm assuming you have read the others to have a clear understanding about the symptoms and implications of bipolar. Having recently struggled though another round of the mental health books from a clinical perspective myself, I've redoubled my efforts to make this a user-friendly, glass-is-half-full perspective. I've also written it for a personal reference book because, even though I know and have practiced all these techniques, remembering them is easier in this format.

There are four parts, beginning with a basic definition, and a brief intro to theory. Part Two is an overview of holistic and preventative body, mind, and spirit techniques. Part Three is a guided tour: "up, down, and back to normal." In Part Four, I share the gifts of being bipolar and describe the opportunity it presents for all of us lucky enough to be bipolar or to know someone who is.

Definitions and Theory
What Is Bipolar?
Good question. It would appear that the more Western science tries to narrow down bipolar, the broader and more complicated it becomes. Some experts even agree that bipolar is more of a spectrum of symptoms and treatments, as opposed to a cut-and-dried, easily identifiable disease. I've also discovered you can spend days getting lost reading all the different theories, definitions, and approaches. It is fascinating and worthwhile, and I highly recommend it. For the purposes of this book, I've boiled down a basic definition in my own words. If you already are bipolar, don't worry about it; in time, you will learn what definition works best for you. The important things to keep in mind are getting help and getting on with your life.

Bipolar disorder, formerly called manic depression, is

a brain disorder. It causes unusual shifts in a person's mood, energy, and ability to function. It is characterized by episodes of mania and depression. It's not the same as the normal ups and downs of life. It can lead to risky behavior and damaged relationships and careers. Between these mood swings, a person with bipolar disorder may experience normal moods. If it's not treated, bipolar disorder can have extreme effects, including risk of suicide.

One other note: bipolar and trauma are a dance often entwined. Some theories surfacing are that bipolar has a latent genetic predisposition which can be triggered by trauma, and then, once set in motion, it stays in motion. It has even been called by some, a chemical reaction to stress. Either way, much is yet to be learned about the discovery and treatment of bipolar.

A Different Definition
I describe the manic phase as visionary. It is a period of time in which we can see potential all around us and in us. We sense dreams, possibilities, and hope. It is endless. Even though we see a panorama of possibilities, not all that we see is true. Without balanced discernment, the perceptions can become psychotic and destructive.

The depressive part of the cycle is an empathy phase. It is a time in which our sensitivity is beyond measure. Our feelings can pick up the slightest perception, real or imagined. We feel deeply all that is incomplete in ourselves, in our group of people, and even in our culture. Left unbalanced, and unstabilized in some way, this state of mind can lead to suicide.

The intense combination of extreme euphoria of human potential and vision with the utter hopeless depths of despair and frustration gives insight to human success and failure. We can see how people dream and succeed in life; we can also completely sympathize with people walking the dark and lonely roads of hopeless failure. This range of human experience inside us leads to a deeper and deeper connection with compassion, and an ever-deepening understanding of human nature and potential are inevitable.

(I've written this definition from a visionary perspective, which is my experience. I believe this same definition can be applied to all of our senses, which are heightened in the bipolar experience.)

Intro to Theory
This is the theory that I have come up with to explain the bipolar experience. If you ever meet a normal person, please let me know I'd like to meet him (or her). But for sake of argument, let's just say a normal person has a fairly regular cycle of ups and downs. He is going to have good days. He is going to have bad days. Some days are better than others.

Now let's introduce a bipolar person. We'll start off with an untreated, unmedicated bipolar person, just raw, right out of the factory. He is going to have extreme highs, and he is going to have extreme lows. He might even have a couple of highs and then a couple of lows; it can be very erratic.

Helicopters
For years, I've tried to figure out how to explain to my mom what the untreated bipolar experience is like. The best metaphor I've come up with yet is that you are blindfolded, riding in a helicopter, going through a storm. You have no clue. You can be cruising along and everything is good, but all of a sudden you are going up or down or all over the place. It can be very disorientating. Some of us grow up thinking everybody is this way. *You mean everyone doesn't feel bleak one minute and on top of the world the next?* Nope, and we don't have to eitheronce we learn how to fly our own minds.

As a helicopter pilot, you need to have situational awareness. You need to know where you are. You need to be able to read your gauges, you need to know if you have enough fuel to be able to get to where you are going, and you need to have a flight plan. You need to have people on the ground, keeping track of where you are.

Have you ever enjoyed a helicopter ride? It's awesome! The pilot is a busy camper. I get to fly in helicopters with my job sometimes, and I've watched the pilots do their thing. It's pretty cool. How a pilot controls the helicopter is very complicated. First of all, he has two foot pedals. These foot pedals control the back of the helicopter, to be able to swing from side to side. The joystick controls the angle at which the helicopter is going to float. He has another control called the collector, which controls going up or down.

Albert Einstein said the definition of insanity is trying the same thing over and over again, expecting different results. An untreated bipolar person starts out blindfolded in the passenger's seat, often feeling like a victim as he goes through the storms or crawls out of the wreck of his life, only to get back in his helicopter, blindfolded again.

This book can help you with the flight school of your mind. It is a guide to finding ways for learning how to use the controls in your 'copter. The better we are at figuring out where we are going (having a dream), learning how to negotiate weather (Life), and reading our gauges (food, mind, and spirit), the sooner some of our swings can mellow out a bit. We can become better at dealing with the biggies when they hit.

Please remove your seatbelt, slide over to the pilot's seat, and begin your journey. Don't worry about the blindfold; this book will help take it off when you're ready.

Part Two
A Holistic Approach

Introduction
In order to get out of the mental institution, they said I had to have a plan for my life. A week before I was locked up, I was interviewed at a strange college down the street which had a body-mind-and-spirit core focus. I really wasn't interested, but it seemed better than walking around in a bathrobe and slippers all day behind bars. It turns out the best thing about that college was their Body, Mind, and Spirit approach. Being very open at the time to try anything other than institutes, I gave it a shot.

Body
Drugs and Alcohol
There is nothing like waking up to the smell of my own stale puke and urine, which I'd been lying in since I passed out. I would open my eyes to look up at an all-too-familiar dumpster, three floors below my apartment and my bed. Those were the good nights, when I almost made it home. The ones that scared me often happened at ten degrees below zero. Something would trigger me, and miles later I'd realize again what I was doing staggering with a bottle of cheap wine along icy roads, wearing only a thin, wool sport jacket. I would walk for hours until my vision narrowed down to a little tunnel in front of me and I would think about the one thing I still cared about: my sister. It was the only way I knew how to deal with and comprehend the pain I felt inside. This was the worst of being bipolar, the negative effects of drugs morphing into a hell I will never forget.

Needless to say, I was a lousy drunk. I usually ended

up locked in a bathroom with people pounding on the door as I curled up around the porcelain god, praying to Ralph. Once I ended up halfway through the bathroom doorway, lying with my pants halfway down, still conscious enough to see the looks of disgust on my friends' faces; I think it was a cheap box wine that night.

I never knew I had blackouts until someone came back after I had sobered up, and he was shocked because I had a respectable job. "I used to drag your butt out of the snowbank, and now you are a resident advisor what's up with that?"

I didn't do any better with dope either. Alaska has a certain valley that produces really potent stuff; I was hooked on it from the beginning. In contrast to alcohol, I could smoke my buddies under the table and then go stare out the window, lost. I'll never forget the night I sucked an eighth through a bong and still felt stone cold sober. I knew it was time to upgrade the drugs to crystal meth like my buddies were doing, or get the hell out while I still could. I had no memory and complete paranoia.

I quit for a while, while I watched my buddies take a fast road down. I ended up using again but eventually was able to quit when I met someone special. I believe she saved my life, because I finally had a reason to live. Fortunately, I had a good support system in place when she moved on, and I survived.

I share this ugliness to let you know why I think self-regulating through drugs and alcohol is the number one thing to get out of if you are bipolar. It only made matters worse for me. The highs were infrequent and extremely out of control, the lows were continuous, and I believe I also robbed myself of the opportunity to complete a degree. I went to college enough years and somehow earned the money to pay for it but was never able to care long enough to stick with a path and do the work.

The untreated reality of bipolar was still the same for me if I wasn't drunk or stoned, which I couldn't afford to be all the time. I was continuously suicidal and paranoid. I was so suicidal, but I couldn't act on the urge. It sucked. All I wanted to do was blow my head off and be done with it, but I was paralyzed. *What if I fucked it up and ended up locked up again?* I hated being behind bars in a mental institution. Country boys like myself are used to roaming wherever we want, and being locked up eliminates all that. Being unable to kill myself because of fear was just like being locked up inside my own body. I hated it: Constant pressure headache. Constant dark thoughts and avoiding people, get to the next class, get to the job, get to the cafeteria. I lived in a triangle job, classroom, dorm. Job for money, class because it kept me from being locked up again, and dorm to get stoned to alleviate the pain of existing.
The long, dark nights of drugs and alcohol had met the worst of the bipolar.

A Way Out …
This might come as a shocker, but I think you're lucky if you have a problem. *Huh?* I don't recommend running

out and picking up a drug habit, but if you already have one, you've just won admission to a worldwide, anonymous support group. The cut-through approach for drug and alcohol abuse is the 12-step programs. What they figured out a long time ago, works, *if you work it.* I went through that route for a number of years. You can proceed with the other areas of your healing, yet if you have a problem with drugs and alcohol, they can destroy your life just as fast as bipolar can.

Even though I thought drugs were "saving" my life at the time by giving me a "break" and allowing me to have a controlled zone-out, they just created more garbage that I had to deal with later. When I was on drugs, I would cycle through swings faster, go higher, stay lower longer, and after a while, I had no life. My short-term memory disappeared, and to this day after many years of sobriety, I'm still having challenges.

There is a suicidal risk with bipolar disorder. Once I sobered up for a while, the numbers of times I thought about suck starting a twelve-gauge reduced greatly, especially once I met my friend Jeff who had and lived to tell about it, sort of.: He shot his wife and daughter through the windshield of a car(they lived), then turned the gun on himself. He was pronounced dead, claims he met and walked with Jesus for awhile, and then came back to tell us about it, powerful message, powerful lesson. I still think of him when my downers are getting ugly. What if I attempt, and I end up like Jeff? It sends shivers up and down my spine. I would love to meet Jesus and any other spiritual guru, yet sometimes I think the natural course of events may be easier.

Another good reason to do 12-steps is because you can go into almost any town anywhere and drop into a group of people who know you. I did that for years. Wherever I traveled, I would freak out my friends because we'd show up in a town I'd never been in, and I'd sneak off to make a few calls (this was before cell phones). Then I'd tell my buddies who were going out to a bar to just drop me off at a meeting place. A couple hours later, I would show back up, usually laughing or peaceful, and they could never figure out why. I'll let you figure it out it if you need to and wish you the best of luck.

Food
Drink a six-pack of Jolt with a buddy, and drive to a truck stop thirty-five miles away on a windy coastal road. Jolt is like a mixture of Mountain Dew and Red Bull on steroids. Driving like an idiot and jabbering at 100 mph about nothing is great fun. It was my favorite kind of study break at college; it was *freedom* from the books. Twenty sledge hammers simultaneously beating on my head while I sat in class trying to remember what I *did* study was severe. Often, huge low swings would be triggered by this, and I'd crawl around like a worm, looking for a tire to finish flattening me.

These were my intense sugar study days. Conclusion: *Stay away from white sugar.* (This is actually a note to self, so that maybe I'll avoid that cheese Danish that is talking to me on the break table). After extensive personal research, including years of no sugar and years of a daily consumption of my favorite gourmet coffee ice cream, it's still on the no-no list when I'm trying to stabilize. Don't worry I've discovered that, once other areas of my life have stabilized, I can consume a reasonable amount of sugar and still feel like crap but not experience the horrendous swings. Officially, *sugar = bad*, especially when I'm feeling unstable.

There is nothing like the nectar of the Gods, I'm referring to coffee of course. Some would say it is evil and bad, they could be right. My experience (remember no degree speaking here), is that caffeine and bipolar, have mixed ok. At times I've jittered way too much and cut back, at times I've avoided it at all costs and discovered a little shot in the morning for a stimulant if I'm immobile and need to exercise has been ok. Bottom line, everyone's body is different, I have no opinions on this one, except of course that %100 Kona, light roast, is IT! It's a smooth buzz I can drink all day and not feel any major swings or burnouts. Enjoy.

A girl I was interested in at college was into a balanced vegetarian diet with supplemental protein. I grew up on meat and potatoes, but she was cute, so I said, *What the heck? I'll try it*. I noticed right away that a lack of "heavy" meat and animal fat in my body knocked off some of the severe highs and lows and brought down the frequency of swings. I thought it was all hocus pocus, so I had several juicy steaks. Sure enough, I would then curl up like a snake and not be as stable for a while. I have since learned that there are many explanations for this, but I won't go into them.

Long after the girl was gone, I ended up living in a residential health center for a while, working in the kitchen. I had access to all different kinds of whole foods and food/mind/body theories, so I used my body as a lab and started experimenting. I learned that what I eat affects how I feel and also influences my energy level. They followed an Ayurveda tradition, which comes from India and has a long tradition of regarding the body from a holistic perspective. To learn more, I recommend studying what they have to offer.

When your mouth opens, and food goes down the hatch, it lands in the stomach. Your stomach does its dance and converts food into what you can use; what you can't use, it passes on down the system. What you can use gets into the bloodstream and finds its way to your brain via your heart. Our brains function better with the right foods. Our brains can help us regulate our emotions and the intensity of our swings.

Here is the tricky part: Everyone is different. Everyone needs different foods and functions better on different eating styles. It is more important to listen to your body and not your mind when it comes to diet. I use my mind to explore and educate myself on all the different options but let my body choose what and when to eat.

A friend, Mike, got it in his head that a certain style of eating was it. He got caught up in it for all the right reasons. He became unbalanced and took his own life. I don't blame the style of eating he chose, because that is not important; it's how he ate, with his mind and not his body, that I believe killed him.

In the mania/visionary phase, we can believe we are right, no matter what. Like my friend, we end up getting lost with that kind of thinking. A big challenge and skill we need to develop and always come back to is listening to our bodies. Our bodies, left unencumbered by what is considered "right" in our heads, can often find balance before our minds can.

Okay, ready for the diet advice? There isn't any. Try different styles, and explore what works best for you. What foods bring you up or down, and which foods keep you stable? What foods work for you best in the morning and at night? How much, and what kind?

Even though it can be uncomfortable eating differently from the people around you at first, over time, if they care about you, they'll notice a positive change in you and become supportive. Believe it or not, even my meat-and-potatoes father admitted once that eating healthy could taste and feel good.

Exercise
One day, I came home, and my ex had spent all my money on a gym membership for the entire family. Yeah, gee, great, I'm exhausted, and now I have to go to the gym? I soon adjusted. I discovered the tanning bed (good for a nap), the hot tub (great place to check out the occasional bikini), and the sauna (antidote for the ungodly cold outside). This, of course, would wear

me out, so I would wander upstairs to the cafeteria for refreshment, the leather couch, and a big screen TV to veg in front of while waiting for the family they always knew where to find me.

Years later, thirty pounds heavier, I actually discovered that people work out at those places. Gyms are actually places where people put on weight in the form of muscle, or take off weight in the form of sweat. Hmmm. I remembered back in junior high when my dad convinced himself that I needed to be an Olympic cross-country skier, and he upgraded my program by making me work out with the high school team. I hated it. I did have six-pack abs and push-ups for punishment were a joke. I'd pop off twenty push-ups when the teachers said to drop and do ten. Back then, I silently admitted to myself that when my body was in shape, my mind felt better. I guess that's why I put up with the long, exhausting hours of keeping my little body going alongside giants otherwise known as high school seniors.

I knew it was time to consider a workout program when, a year after my divorce, women were no longer the motivating factor for looking good. You'll never guess, so I'll tell you. The trigger was putting on my boots. I have to wear steel-toe boots for work. We have to take them off whenever we go in or out of the living quarters. It was a three-step process. Fall down on bench. Push stomach over to one side. Exhale as much air as possible, and then, again, get down to the laces and tie the boots. Twice a day or more, I would have to go through this ordeal. Let's just say that my mind was in similar shape. Of course, I had tried every diet in the known universe. But exercise? God forbid. But the time had come, and I knew. Next time I was in town, I bought a new pair of my favorite sneakers and a matching brand name outfit to go with it. Hey, if I'm going to be fat at a gym, I'm going to look good doing it. Off to the gym I went. About three months later, I had to use a pillow instead of my belly to snuggle up with at night because the belly was no longer available. Soon, blood visited my brain on a regular basis again, and my attitude improved. Now my boots are easy to put on, and I still chuckle when I remember what a chore it used to be.

The biggest trick I've found to avoid catatonic couch time is to live in an environment in which it is easy to exercise. For me, bike riding and walking on the beach are the best ways to exercise. So be it, even though it took a couple years and, in the meantime, I had to join a gym, now that I live near the ocean, it is so much easier to exercise regularly.

While physical exercise is not a cure for bipolar, it is a building block we can use to support ourselves. It is not an instant fix either. It takes regular daily effort. No insta-fixes. It's not important how many times I quit exercising or how lazy I get. What's important is how many times I start again. Not only is this important, so that I don't focus on my failures in physical exercise, but it also emphasizes the importance of picking myself up and trying again. With bipolar, we are going to have ups and downs. The better we get at picking up after downs and focusing on what worked and on what we did right, and starting again, the sooner we can begin to gain some long-term stability. It may seem like inches in a strong headwind, but over time, with a positive focus, we begin to gain traction and see progress.

I have found, through experiencing a body that is in good physical shape, that it is easier for me to identify earlier subtle changes that signal a swing. Exercise is also a healthy outlet for stress before it becomes a trigger. The biggest benefit I've found when I'm in shape and a swing has occurred, is the ability to stabilize more quickly. I don't know the scientific explanation for this; I just know it works.

The exercise and discipline that I have found the most effective is Hatha yoga. Yoga is simple and effective, and it has been around for thousands of years. *Okay, yeah, right. What's going to happen next, Denslow? My legs are going to be crossed, and I'll be chanting* ommm? … Um, well, that's what happened to me. And, yes, at one point this morning in class, I was in a half-lotus position, and I chanted *om*. Guilty. And full of a big *ahhhh*. Yoga does for my mind and body what marijuana used to do for me. It helps me totally relax. After a yoga class, I can drive home much faster without the cops pulling me over asking me why I'm driving 5 mph, even though my mind would be convinced I was driving 80 while "relaxing" on marijuana.

I was introduced to yoga at my first weeklong spiritual retreat. I learned a little routine called the sun salutation. It can be completed really fast or slowly; I do about three every morning. I've done them everywhere parking lots, snowstorms, beaches. Part of my motivation was a bad back that used to go out on me all the time and prevent me from working. After a while, I noticed that my back was okay, I was more flexible, had less pain, and, again, my swings lessoned and my high and lows were no longer as severe. Nowadays, you can find yoga DVDs at most department stores or online. Buy one, and check it out. If you like it, go find a buddy or a class that does yoga, and enjoy!

Okay, honesty time here. The more stable and at peace I feel in my mind and life, the less likely I am to exercise and eat right. This usually leads to lows, but not severe lows. Periodically, from time to time, I've had enough, and I get in shape again. I've beat myself up for years over this. The important thing is that I know it works, and I do it when I've had enough of feeling fat, or the swings get a little more frequent than I'm comfortable with. Ideally, we'd all be fitness buffs and never have to watch our waists go up and down the scale; what's more practical is enjoying stability and progress in our lives, even if we aren't physically "perfect." Exercise is also just another tool in the box for stabilizing and at times can be an obsession too; we can get into overzealous, unhealthy mental states in just about anything. Finding the balance is the art form. Identifying the safe, healthy routines to come back to is the beginning of reasonable stability.

Is It Open for Hugs?
Okay, Mom, this one is for you. I love you. Thanks for all the hugs, and is it still open? I don't know when I figured

this one out but it is a surefire method for getting extra loving when needed. I'm told that, at an early age, I used to tilt my head, look up, open my arms, and ask, "Is it open for hugs?" Sometimes words just didn't cut it. So I would ask for what I needed. I can still remember that *ahhh* I would get when big loving arms would embrace me, and I could feel the warmth of another human. I don't think much has changed since then. I still use that line.

Bipolar is a constant 24/7 job. If the helicopter scenario doesn't quite fit, try this one. You are in a plane, flying on autopilot. Your brain is functioning normally, getting from point A to B through life. All of a sudden, the autopilot quits working, and you don't remember how to fly. It doesn't mean you can't. Nothing is inherently wrong with the plane or your brain. One system is down, that's all. This book and others like it can help you remember how to fly again. In the process, get lots of hugs. Why? Because it is okay to be scared. Hugs can help you get through the moment and on to your next opportunity to help yourself heal.

Massage
It is easy to become physically isolated from the human race. Trust me on this, from having spent more years of my adult life living alone than with someone. A majority of this has been out of choice because of the focus on my journey of healing. The times that have not been from conscious choice emerged from a lack of trust and knowing how I would be with someone. How long would someone put up with my mood swings before

they would move on? Bipolar can be rough on long-term relationships. It is easy for us to run away, not wanting to cause pain in someone's life and not feeling the pain in ourselves. If this is happening, and there is any way you can manifest it in your life, get massage, even if it's only once a month. Get touched by a licensed professional.

In the electronics field that I work in, after a certain number of errors, alarms will lock out in a high or low state, which means a system can shut down or not function properly. In a similar way, so many alarm bells go off inside of us when things are not normal. Massage is a great way to reset all of our alarms and help us to relax and accept everything in our life just the way it is, even for a moment. Many times, I've been stressed out beyond measure, spooling up for another all-nighter with nothing to do or freaking out about some unresolved issue. I've had a massage instead, and suddenly things are okay again for a while, and I can see a resolution I didn't see before. I am able to get a full night's sleep and be more fully functional the next day. Try it you'll love it.

Snuggle Buddies
No, "snuggle buddies" not about or a precursor to sex. Clothes must remain on. Clear boundaries must be established or else the safety and deep nurturing is not effective. Words are not necessary or required; in fact, they are discouraged. Recommended daily dosage: at least once a day for twenty minutes with a trusted friend. I don't have any academic degrees in this area, but I'm willing to bet a year's pay, that if everyone could get twenty minutes of calm, gentle physical contact with a

safe person every day, then drug companies would be out of business. Find someone you trust, and explain to them your situation and desire to hold and be held. Explain the ground rules where it is okay to be held and where it is not, and for how long, and that it is not about sex, it's about physical nurturing.

I don't know the technical terms; I just know it works. Our physical bodies can calm down, and soon our minds will follow. Likewise, if we are depressed and are held for a while, chances are, we will feel better able to take care of ourselves afterward. If we abuse this privilege with someone by needing or wanting too much, then that doesn't work either. Make sure you talk it through before, during, and after, to establish and maintain clear boundaries for you and your buddy.

If this works for you, then welcome to Wally's Snuggle Buddy Club. (Wally is my happy inner kiddo.) Please join Wally and me in our quest to visualize and manifest volunteer snuggle buddy clubs anywhere they are needed. They would be official, privately funded, and operated by a trained volunteer staff in a safe, open, supervised atmosphere in which anyone with appropriate behavior could give or receive a snuggle. Yeah, sure, what a goofy idea, but just wait you'll love it. You are in a big, strange city, far from loved ones, and you are experiencing anxiety or loneliness. You go to the nearest registered snuggle buddy club, get a snuggle, and go about your business with a big *ahh*.

Or you are lonely, have been alone for years, and finally

get up the courage to go to a snuggle buddy club. You feel relief immediately and set up a daily appointment for twenty minutes (recommended dosage, although you still have to deal with why you find yourself anxious) and begin changing your life in a positive direction. Maybe you even become a snuggle buddy club volunteer.

There is not a lack of love or help; it's merely our imaginations that are limiting us from being able to connect in safe and appropriate ways in order for us to receive the help we need and improve the quality of our lives. The inspiration for this comes from the years in which I was a lost male in our society. I could go for years, literally, without being touched. I was dealing with deep, dark inner agony, and I knew I needed touch but did not have the words or safe opportunities to create it. If we could get help to men and women in the same condition that I was in, much darkness could be lifted from our culture. Enough said now go snuggle; in fact, I think it's time for my 4 PM snuggle. *Where is she? Ahhh.*

Mind
Intro to Counseling
I took acid in a state I had never been in, in a group where I only knew only one person, and then I went to a party. All of a sudden, what I had taken for granted as tangible reality melted into a wavy universe. You think your mind goes fast, now, holy cow, Batman! It was extreme hyperdrive. At one point, long after the party went away, or I went away from the strange creatures, I thought, *Okay, cool, I'm on acid. Let's go to the moon.* Instant bingo, I was on the surface of the moon, looking

back at earth. The problem was, my mind kept thinking. Instantly, I was eating a burrito, then under the oceans, looking at monsters coming out of a closet, then at cars driving through a window, while I was attempting to have a conversation. It was endless. Whatever I thought I had was instantly manifested in my imagination. Before I could enjoy it, the next thought was there.

I use this extreme example of my demonstrated stupidity, to illustrate the power of our minds. Whatever we focus on, increases. That which is happening right now, matters. This moment has the greatest effect on my life. Not yesterday, not tomorrow.

I was in a dark space when this journey began, with every justifiable reason to quit before I ever started. A decision had to be made. I shut the door to my past and moved on. I said, *Oh well, life goes on.* With all the things that had happened and all the things that were "wrong" with me, according to my estimation and that of others, I realized that I had to focus on the solution. The problems were simply too overwhelming and energy-draining. What mental energy I had left, I focused on today, right here, and right now. What could I do to help make things better? It's not uncommon to have things go well for a while and then crash again. Crashing is not so important, but getting up from the wreck and focusing on the solution is.

I have found there is a time and a place for looking at the past. Many insights can be revealed, to help you through your present dilemmas, but going into your own mind and history without a guide is not recommended. I say this after years of avoiding counseling and trying everything else but. Certainly, I've uncovered and discovered many things and have made a lot of progress and had quite a few adventures on my own. But I can see now where finding a good counselor in the beginning could have avoided quite a few pitfalls. This is why I emphasize counseling as the number one priority, in this section of the book.

Everything else I list is important and has helped me immensely and has certainly kept me alive and functioning. I have found that ignoring the core crap that happened at a young age is like swimming a marathon in a cold lake, getting to the dock, and someone hands you an engine block, or is nice enough to point out you've been swimming with one. We can adapt really well to patterns of behavior that are not of benefit to us anymore. It is like carrying around a heavy load(engine block), and not noticing anymore how much we have to compensate for the extra weight or how much more exhausted we are for coping with it.

My early successes with counseling were limited. My first counselor locked me up with a good and valid intent I didn't see at the time. Others were in the mental institute, and I never trusted or saw them again. The last one I tried would listen, open me up as if for brain surgery, and then forget to put the pieces back before the hour was up. It was my last attempt for over ten years.
Counseling has come a long way, and I encourage you to keep trying it out till you find a counselor who works and

then dig in. It could save you a lot of years of heartbreak.

The metaphor I like the best for counseling is if you think of all the kings and queens throughout history, they all had advisors, so my counselor is my advisor. It is a wonderful, wonderful thing to have a conscious human being looking at your babble and guiding you. Counseling is a vital element, even just for an evaluation or a checkup. Maybe you'll get a clean bill of mental health and not worry about it, but a lot of our triggers are known and can be worked with through talking. Why not get them out of the way now instead of waiting years like I did? Old stuff can be cleared up, and new stuff can be alleviated before it becomes a problem.

Always Have an Exit Plan
Being the emotional and energy-influenced creatures that we are, incessant self-counseling and diagnosis are traps we can lose ourselves in. Whenever I find myself focusing on trying to figure me out way more than is appropriate, I kick in the exit plan. There is always a present in the present. I focus on the day, my current physical sensations, and actively get involved with what I'm doing. If it is rote and boring, and safe to think about something else, I try and focus on my next goal or project, anything to get me out of me, and into something bigger and safer until the time is appropriate to focus again within.

If I am balanced and adventurous, or a path opens up in front of me through quiet contemplation that seems right, then I can explore the uncomfortable negativity within a little bit. Gently, I may look at my current situation, and allow insights to bubble up. If they seem to provide clarity into a situation or my body relaxes and releases stress, I trust them. If overwhelming anxiety or my body tightens up, then I'm not ready to explore this alone, yet. When it's time to move on, my favorite saying is to repeat what day, month, and year it is, over and over again until I can find something positive about right now, like the feeling of good clean clothes, a meal, or even just breathing. Then I try and obsess about this positive aspect of my day, until I can move on to the next best action.

Abuse
Abuse in any form is not fun. Being the extremely sensitive, aware creatures that we naturally are, from knowing the highs and lows of life, any real or perceived abuse revealed in counseling can be a bit unstabilizing to take on.

Let me just stop everything, reach out through this book, and give you a big hug. I won't go into details, but I will say that I manifested my share of darkness from others in this life too. Some of it has been devastating to uncover and very horrendous to live through again until healed.

My heart is with you right now. I can assure you that each discovery I have made, shared with a trusted friend or counselor, and worked through has led to a whole new level of mental freedom, empathy, and understanding of life. It has eased my lows a bit and made my highs more calmly enjoyable. It has also given me the mental stability to be able to go after my dreams in a calm and focused manner, which I didn't think was possible.

In the dark cave of victimhood, this may not be what you want to hear. Please know that I've curled up in a ball and soaked more than one pillow and drained a few counselors' tissue boxes, and left snotty rags in inconvenient places. Hang in there, Buddy, because we need you. We want you to make it through and succeed, so we can know you and your visions. You have something to offer that we haven't seen, heard, or known yet. Even if you don't know it yet, the very thing you may be crawling through right now may lead you to a spark for the rest of your life. Whatever it is, please don't let it stop you from sharing your life with us.

Journaling
Why journal?
Believe it or not, there is more room on the outside of our brains than there is on the inside.
If our brains were Ferris wheels, and we fill them up with thoughts, or people riding in the chairs, and don't let them off now and then to take care of business, we'll soon have a mess on our hands.

Yes, it gets stinky. Journaling is letting the people (our thoughts) off the Ferris wheel (our minds) on a regular basis so that we can get new thoughts and not let olds ones get trapped and fester ideas that no longer serve our best interests.

When our brains have regularly allowed our ideas to get on paper, we free our Ferris wheels to explore life with new ideas and people and actually go somewhere. We can also look back where we have been, and look forward to where we want to go. It's exciting to have a fresh mind full of new ideas and people. Journaling is one method for allowing this to happen.

Or we can just get up every day and, chances are, see parts of the same day we saw before and wonder why our lives are going around in smelly circles instead of actually getting somewhere.

Now
First, it's important to know where we have been. With bipolar, it's so easy to get caught up in the bumpy boat ride and forget everything else that has ever happened. Our drama can be so traumatic that we don't even bother to pay attention to it anymore. If you want some of the drama to dissipate and want to begin to slow down the ride, you can begin by capturing what's going on now in your brain.

Sometimes, when I'm all wound up, I walk in circles in my office because I don't have time to sit, yet I can't sort out the priorities to actually go in a direction that will accomplish something. I like to call these train wrecks, caused by too many trains going into the station and not enough coming out. I'll force myself to sit down, grab a sheet of paper, and write in the middle of it the first word or issue that comes to mind. And then another and another. Sometimes this takes two or three sheets, but that's okay. Sometimes they are a repeat, and that's okay.

The more thoughts I get on paper, the more room I get in the train station in my brain, and I can begin to see what's going on. I may have a work priority heading in this direction, a personal item going in another, a time crunch over here, or I'm hungry, and yet what's really bothering me is a comment from a friend or loved one that I feel like I need to take a moment to support. Bingo, sometimes this is all it takes. I can take a moment to do what is important which is not necessarily what I *need* to do right now but it still is what's important. I can call or e-mail the friend, and then I'm okay. Maybe the friend needed to talk to me, or maybe I needed to hear his or her voice. I don't know, and I don't try to figure these things out anymore; life just seems to work better when I pay attention to these opportunities. Afterward, an order appears out of the chaos, and I can move on to the next task.

That's journaling in the now.

Past

If feelings or memories come up from the past or if there are some that keep spinning around in your head, it's good to get these out on paper too. It creates more space and frees up head traffic for the next rush hour. This is also very helpful if you are in counseling; helpful life lessons can be extracted, and then you don't have to keep thinking about them any more. I try not to dwell on the past too much. I like to let it bubble up on its own, because then it seems to have the energy needed to deal with it, and I don't get lost trying to figure it all out or change it.

Future
Here is the fun part. It's the beginning of your new life and dreams. Your pen is your magic wand, and your canvas is your paper. What do you love? What did you like to do as a kid? What do you want to do right now? Record or draw these things on paper, and put the notes someplace where you see them every day. I highly recommend the fridge; it keeps working for me.

Daily
Writing a couple of pages every day enables us to wake up, shake out the cobwebs, and begin the day without extra chatter from the night, clouding up the airways. We may wake up thinking we are fine, yet pen and paper can bring out something bothering us, and we can take care of it right away instead of waiting till it makes a mess. Or we may wake up grumpy, but a few words or affirmations later, we have averted a downer day.

We are so sensitive to feelings, energies, and emotions of others. It is really good to check in on a regular basis. If you are rooted and know where you are, you can be less susceptible to someone else's agenda other than your own, plus you can feel like you have a positive direction. It's like driving down an unpaved road. At 35 to 40 mph, you can feel every bump. If you can safely take it up to 80 mph, your tires go across the tops of the bumps, and the ride smoothes out. This, of course, is an extreme example, but you can get my point: if your mind is going somewhere, then you are less likely to get caught up in every possible swing.

After-action Reports
Journaling serves another purpose for the bipolar person:; developing a personal mental health history. As we take the time to write, our ups, our downs, and everything else in between, we are developing a continuum that doesn't naturally come from within us. It's so easy to forget all that is going on inside of us, so; it can be very helpful to have a reference written in our own hand to go back to and try to figure out what happened.

If we are just crawling out of a depression, or recovering from a manic, we can go back and look at our mental state before hand. We might discover what triggered us, and be wary in the future. We might also see what we could have done differently. Like call our friends before we drink the fifth of rum. Over time, this becomes a preventative measure. The more we write, the less swells up in our head to trigger a swing, and when we see triggers on paper, before they happen, we can think about possible consequences.

We are beginning to be given a choice , *do I really want to go crazy right now, or do I like my job, car, girlfriend, and [fill in the blank]?*. What usually disappears first? If we are starting to take really good care of ourselves and have a few dreams we are looking forward to and actually working on, we may choose to take corrective measures first. If we have never had a "life,", and we finally start to develop one, then journaling is a really good technique we can include in our daily routine to help smooth out the ride and avert possible catastrophes.

If we do pop a gasket and find ourselves riding our bicycles down busy streets on acid (oops, sorry, having a flashback here), then it's sometimes fun to record our adventures (it's okay to cry too), so that, next time we can have even more information to review before popping the cork and wondering where we will end up this time.

This, Too, Shall Pass
I almost forgot journaling proves, without a doubt, that no matter what we are going through, good or bad, this, too, shall pass. At dark points in my life, I have sat down, usually late at night, still worried about the next day. During one of these sleepless nights, I was rummaging around and found an old journal. It was horrible. Whine, whine, whine. I was embarrassed to read my own ramblings, yet I saw something: that which I had been so upset with, had now successfully passed to a resolution, one way or another. Also, I was now living some of the dreams, visions, and longings I had been writing about, after hoping that all the spiritual and feel-good books were true.

What a miracle my journals showed me that night, and what a technique was revealed. Now, when I have a worrisome, sleepless night, I try and sit back and reflect where I was a year ago. What were my problems and dreams? Then, I look back at today. Did anything change from a year ago? Usually, life has gotten better in some way. Once I've gone back far enough to see the fruits of my labor, which resulted in my current day, coming from my past, then I'll look at what I did today. Did I do my healthy daily routine? Did I spend time focusing on my current dreams and taking baby steps or leaps toward them? Okay, great, now here is the fun part. I look ahead. What if I kept doing these little steps each day for one year? Where might I be? Wow. Remember our overactive imaginations? Yeah, use 'em for good. Many times now, many darks nights, I've used this technique, and not only did I get through the night and have courage to get through the next day, many times I've looked back at these very nights a year or more later and thanked myself for taking the time to visualize in detail the current dream I was now living. Don't be bashful it's your life, create it!

Books A Way Out
In ancient times, when a special child was born, he or she was identified by the elders and passed on to the tutelage of the local shaman. Through the discovery and training of the child's special gifts, the tribe would, in turn, receive benefits from the individual care given to the child who didn't fit the mold. Thousands of years later, a tribe might use drugs to try to control the child's behavior instead of seeking out the truths and providing extra attention in order to receive the gifts of "special" children who don't fit the mold. It is a full cycle. As the child is provided for, so the child shall be better prepared and able to serve the tribe in return. This is not convenient in modern times, because we believe in better living through chemicals.

Fortunately, much of the ancient wisdom is becoming available to us through books and teachers. The special attention is not individualized and offered at birth, but we are getting there. This is why, as soon as you become aware of your special gift of being bipolar, it is important to begin your spiritual journey. A doorway to this journey is through the education of your mind. If your mind can become open to both the new and ancient ways of being, then your rhythms, however great and frequent they are, can begin to make more sense. This is how it happened for me.

I admit it. She was cute, happened to be my first girlfriend, and she gave me my first "spiritual" book to read. *Of course*, I read it. Wow, thank God I did. This guy made sense to me. Things I intuitively knew about life, yet had never heard or read about anywhere were on paper in a book. What a flipping discovery. What a relief. Someone, somewhere, had described my interior life and led me farther down a path I knew felt good. I was getting relief from mental and spiritual anguish I didn't know I had, by reading a book.

Books are vital to our existence when dealing with bipolar. Here is why: Untreated bipolar is like listening to static on the radio in between stations. Nothing makes sense. Reading positive spiritual books can help us to understand our highs. Some people may have one or more spiritual highs in their life. Some people only go through one or two dark nights of the soul. But some of us at times can experience this as a daily reality. Positive spiritual books give the mind information about your perspective when you are low and can help alleviate any attitudes that aren't part of your organic empathetic rhythm. Books can also help describe a practical way of being in and enjoying the high place of vision.

You can be in the presence of your creator and begin to be grounded at the same time. If you have practical knowledge of spiritual highs, they can be less scary. If you have tools and techniques for grounding your visions and dreams, then you can feel less crazy and more able to work toward bringing them to reality. Without this information from books, the bipolar experience can make you nervous and anxious when you are high, and dark and hopeless when you are down.

As with all things that I get a healthy charge from, I was soon buying this book and that, reading all the time, and couldn't go anywhere without a backpack full of books. Why? Because after reading a positive truth that hit home, my body would breathe a big sigh of relief. Just like with meditation, healthy books were giving me a pause in my perspective of life. Some of the big, dark uglies from my past, which I had shut out, were resurfacing again. Through reading positive-perspective books, I was beginning to get the notion that there was a silver lining.

I don't mention which ones I've read because there is an abundant ever evolving supply of excellent authors and positive perspectives. The ones I was drawn to or given may not be the ones you need. I trust intuition to guide me to what I need to read, whether it is a line in a trash novel or a modern positive metaphysical book. When in doubt I always turn back to the tried and true ancient texts, my favorite is <u>The Tao Te Ching</u>, by Lao Tzu.

Maybe I need to describe my life at that time a little better. I was rapid cycling, suicidal on a moment-by-moment basis and extremely paranoid about being locked up again. At the drop of a hat, something could trigger a reaction in me, and I would literally be miles away, out of breath, before I knew what happened. This had been my daily reality for a couple of years. Granted, the drugs and alcohol weren't helping any, but even after I had sobered up and was working a good program, I was still having these reactions.

The books I read were a lifeline to my existence. When I read them, for the moment, I wasn't "crazy." When they started to work on my perspective, and my constant "craziness" started to dissipate, I knew a miracle was happening in my life. It's no surprise that when an author of one of the books I was reading came to town and gave a presentation, I went. Six months later, he was giving a weeklong retreat in Hawaii. You must understand, I was broke, earning minimum wage, and working my way through college. I somehow came up with the money and went.

A year or so later, I was in my room, attempting to study books that I was paying good money for, to learn and get an education. I was looking up at the set of books that I had bought that were leading me out of my darkness into a new and happy life. It was a no-brainer. I quit school and began my spiritual quest. I had to find out for myself, beyond a shadow of a doubt, just how accessible this feel-good, higher power/self stuff was.

Eventually, life moved on, and I was in a dark space again. Many good things had happened, but when some of the garbage underneath bubbled up again, I turned to the books. This time, while reading them, I noticed that, no matter how bad or dark my days were, if I took the time in the morning and at night five or ten minutes to read, then my mind had something else besides my problems to chew on all day. In the darkest times, when I had lost connection with my positive spirit, I noticed my mind would keep working, even if I was catatonic on my couch. I could lie there and watch my mind remember truths I had read that morning. They would filter through and help me unsort the moment. On days when I skipped reading, it was more like watching nightmare reruns, and it would take much longer before I was functional again.

Books have shortened the lag time between struggling with life lessons and moving through them, by enabling me to follow a path someone discovered before me. I may beat on a problem for years, yet seeking the help of others' experiences through books changes my perception in some way, and then the problem often goes away, or I'm okay with the situation, and it doesn't bug me anymore.

Books, books, books, everywhere. Here is what I also discovered, which could save you some money and maybe help you stay in school and get a degree. After a while, it didn't seem to matter what book I had with me or what page I turned to what I needed at the time showed up on the pages. Hmmm. I saw this and made a decision.

Instead of having ten books with a zillion bookmarks and

intentions to finish them all, I picked one (my first) and carried it around with me like a bible for a year. I studied it in depth. I highlighted it. I wrote out sections and put them on my walls everywhere. I didn't care; whatever space was mine at work or home, I would put a truth or some words of wisdom on it. Every challenge, upset, or question I had, I would open the book up and read until I was calm and focused again or in some way alleviated. It didn't always work, but most of the time, within a day, the answers would come, and I would be okay again for a while. This did me a great service and was the beginning of my spiritual strength.

Here is the update. I'm jealous. I ended up dropping out of college to read and pursue my life by reading a lot of books that have now found their way into college courses and degrees. Go figure but it's good news. If what you are studying now isn't cutting it for you, consider a degree in metaphysics because you already have a leg up on the competition. Bipolar is living metaphysics. I keep getting ahead of myself.

This section of my book would not be complete if I didn't thank my teacher, the one who led me out of my darkness and back into the light inside me: thank you, Alan. May the truth you taught me in my time of darkness take the form it needs to through me, to continue the chain of light, reaching out to people still existing in their own hell.

Music Brainwash Anyone?
It wouldn't be fair to appreciate my spiritual teacher

without mentioning the guy who bypassed my dark mind and went into my heart through his words and music. He happened to be the cohort of Alan at the time, with the first and second workshop I went to. Let's just say my musical collection at the time leaned toward the macho, tough guy, preferably played loud and listened to while drunk, in order to fully appreciate it.

Here comes this guy with an acoustic guitar and loving, gentle lyrics. Eeuuuuu. No, no, I'm melting. I'll lose my masculinity. Yeah, right, b.s. Remember garbage in, garbage out? Music affects us in spite of our minds. Just like the books, when I listened to this guy's stuff instead of headbanger music, I stopped beating my head on the walls (literally). Did anyone mention yet that we have a tendency to go to extremes?

Okay, here is another one that could save you a chunk of money. Yep, you guessed it: I felt good, so I gave away my entire music collection. All I did was listen to feel good music and read positive spiritual books for a year. Wow, what a brainwashing that was. Here is why.

What are your beliefs? What reactions does your mind operate from? What inner values do you agree with? Do they support your need to have a positive focus in your life? Are your perceptions of interactions with others and your reflections of your own past accurate? Is it possible that a positive force may exist in the universe that conspires to help you with your dreams?

Deep inside, by watching how negative I was most of the

time, and seeing how much good was coming into my life from the positive "brain food" I was now giving it, I made the decision to brainwash myself. Dealing with bipolar is enough of a challenge on its own. I could see that having a positive attitude and perspective was helping out immensely.

Being willing to go to any length to get better and support my journey is vital. Do I have regrets? Yeah, sure, I can't remember what all the headbanger music was, but does it really matter? Am I a constantly glazed-over Pollyanna? No, but I now have internal positive reactions that kick in along with the old programming that's still present, and this puts me in a positive direction no matter what challenge I'm facing.

Life is going to bring us lemons. The more positive problem-solving skills we provide ourselves with to help keep a positive focus, the less likely that new challenges can trigger a swing or send us running into a high or low state to avoid what's really going on.

Remember: I don't mention whom I listened to, and I'm not selling any music, so I'm not the one brainwashing you. What you brainwash yourself with is up to you. I'm just asking questions. How positive, and to what length are you willing to go to clean your brain out and infuse it with good vibes?

P.S. Don't give away your collection; just put it in storage.
P.S.S. Thanks, Charley. I'm still dancing in the light.

Workshops
How was the brainwash? Feel good? Great! Are you ready for more? I assume by now you've found a spiritual author or teacher you like. Go online and find out where and when they are presenting next. Go.

Spiritual workshops are full of like-minded people on similar paths, and I've always found them to be receptive to me, no matter how I showed up, literally and figuratively. There have been occasions where I've observed blowouts by people struggling with their mental gifts and have witnessed success stories with incredible healings. To be fair, I've also witnessed individuals being asked to leave.

Every human potential workshop I have ever attended has altered the course of my life in a positive direction. After my first weeklong workshop, a chunk of the universe healed inside of me. I came home. I curled up in a little ball, and slept like a baby for a week. I felt innocent, pure, clean, and whole. I had no idea of the worry and residual fear I was living with on a daily basis that had accumulated inside of me from growing up with bipolar.

Bipolar can take its toll on our self-esteem. It's important to receive love and appreciation from others in a safe environment until we can provide this for ourselves. Workshops let us practice loving and accepting ourselves with others so that when we go back into the world, we stand a chance of taking better care of ourselves, using the new skills we learn.

Workshops are *usually* a safe environment to go deeper and have emotional releases, which reinforce the new truths we are discovering about ourselves and our past. The more we can learn to love and accept ourselves, *no matter what*, the sooner we can accept our present condition, and maybe even one day leave it behind us too ; >.

A word of caution: all that love and attention is a surefire way of triggering a high and an addiction. I know this from firsthand experience. Always tell your loved ones before you go, and be prepared for coming off the feel-good high when you come home. Let people know beforehand that you might experience a downer when you come back, and then you could use some extra support. Also, make sure you get e-mails and keep in contact with your new buddies. If possible, connect up with some local people to go with you, or meet someone from your area while you are there. Don't be afraid to mention to the workshop leader where you are at with your "gifts" you might find that person to be very supportive. If, in the rare situation, he or she is not, then maybe it is not a workshop you need to attend. Spiritual workshops and retreats are a warm and fuzzy treat you are worthy of. Treat yourself as often as you can. Scholarships and volunteer opportunities are often available. I was never afraid to wash dishes, in order to hear gifts from a true healer.

Head Banging to Mozart by the River
Lift off, I'm pissed. @#$%$ this job/marriage/

relationship/person/place. Get the picture? Yep, I know been there, done that, right? Hey, guess what? Me too. One day, I was recklessly driving my '92 Eagle Summit (4-door compact economy car) like a monster truck through a favorite mudhole. I was jamming out to a favorite standard, AC/DC's "Back in Black." Sometimes, no other album will do it for me. It takes me back to being 16. I was living on my own, working at a car wash to support myself, and still trying to drag myself through high school. I couldn't think of any other reason to live other than to wake up and turn up the volume. When the screaming, obnoxious rock would perform CPR on my heart, and the lyrics cut through the pain of my existence, I felt alive and okay. Someone knew at some point what I was going through and why.

Anyway, back in the '92 Summit. I had discovered, even though my clearance was very low and my tires were small, with only myself in the car at very high speeds, I could go over the surface of the mud and not get stuck, if I didn't stall out in the water holes. I've often abused and used cars as a disposable item for my driving pleasure. I was well into my thirties before a car I owned ever made it past the first year without blowing out a transmission.

In the midst of all this, I put a slightly less obnoxious CD into the player by accident. I had been jamming out for a while, feeling the rush of not quite getting stuck in mud, while chunks of glob were covering my windshield. I thought I was still pissed off, but I was able to tolerate the slightly less obnoxious music. Hmm. I thought, *Wait a minute. I really don't like loud hard rock all that much anymore yet it seems to work for anger, yet now I'm not as angry and I can tolerate this other stuff.*

I conducted an experiment. Female voices can sometimes take the edge off anger even more if I've gone through the initial phases, so I tried one of my favorites. It worked. I was a little less on edge. I made a few more jumps with my car, found my way to a favorite hidden spot on the river, and got even bolder. I put in some Mozart. Wow. Maybe this is what they call music therapy.

Instead of continuing to pound my head, blow out my eardrums, and beat up my car, I was able to go from a hate-my-life/job bad day blow out, to Mozart on the river, in a couple of hours, and I didn't quit my job that day. On many occasions since then, I've tried it successfully. I haven't lost any transmissions in a couple years; in fact, I was actually able to sell my last truck and not turn it into the scrap heap. Music can help us match our energy and emotions wherever we are and bring us carefully, notch by notch, back to a friendlier place in our minds. Enjoy!

Meditation
I was introduced to meditation while taking karate classes. As I walked around my first year at college, I knew two things, I was extremely paranoid of being locked up again, and extremely angry. The idea came to me to take karate classes. It was inevitable I was going to get into a fight so I might as well learn how to defend myself. Funny how spirit works. They offered classes in Kokondo on campus. Kokondo is based on self-defense,

not competition. The whole point was to practice our skills so that we never needed to hurt or be hurt. This was also my intro to meditation a simple ten minutes a day, sitting quietly and breathing.

Why meditation? It's an impressive, subtle tool, we can use. Our normal reactions to life are pretty much automatic. We bounce along and don't really notice much or how the world affects us. Bipolar is all about emotions and energy levels inside of us. If we aren't aware of what's going on around us or how it affects us inside, then we are just the ball in a pinball machine.

Meditation is actually very simple. People love to complicate it, like everything else, and convince us that one way is better than another, but let me break it down really simply: just sit and breathe. (Yes, I actually went to China and heard this from a Taoist teacher.) Here is my simple approach. Get a minute-hand watch or clock and stare at it for one full minute. That's a great beginning. Just the act of forcing yourself to slow down and not physically react to every thought or impulse is powerful. Start out with one minute a day, and work your way up to ten. Observe and write down any differences you may feel. At first, you may not notice a difference. Another easy way to get into meditation is through guided meditations, of which you can find many at your local bookstore.

Over time, I noticed that, instead of a direct line from my brain to my mouth or body, there was a pause. It was a miracle. Instead of thinking and telling someone they were a complete idiot and getting us both worked up, I noticed that there was a thought, a pause, and then I would call them an idiot. Eventually, through meditation, I was able to begin slowing my mind down enough to decide that I really didn't need to call as many people idiots anymore, and I could begin focusing my energies instead at understanding the situation instead of fighting it.

This is a big piece for dealing with a manic phase. I was beginning to notice what would spool up my energy and emotions, and I would be able to calm them down before things got out of hand. I was also able to wake up sooner in the middle of a manic phase, realize what I was doing, and force myself to take a time out. Sit down, read a daily book, and breathe for one minute or ten. This technique was responsible for my being able to hold a job for longer than six months.

If you do get serious about meditation, I strongly recommend you find a formal teacher and practice and a support group to do it with. It's also not a bad idea to sign up for counseling as well. The reason is simple. When we begin to slow our minds down, we begin to see our inner demons, secrets, and that which we would rather avoid. It can be very uncomfortable, and many people quit. If we stick with and work through these issues as they come up, we can actually lessen the reasons to increase or decrease our swings unconsciously.

Energy, Rhythm, Vision
Along the pipeline in remote Alaska are many water

crossings in order to access the maintenance road. For years, the crew came along and straightened out the creek to make a crossing point. Each spring, water would wipe out the access road, and in early summer they would have to rebuild it. Finally, someone came along and pointed out that the river seems to want to go this way, so why don't we design an access point that doesn't disrupt the natural flow of the river? They tried it. They went upstream, took pictures of the way the river usually took its bends, and designed a crossing that took this into account. Guess what? The next spring, the access road didn't wash out. The river was able to maintain its natural rhythm through the area and to ignore all the trucks splashing through.

)(*&@#$

Okay, I've had enough of this, Denslow. Where is all this leading to? I'll tell you. It's about energy, rhythm, and vision. If you take care of your body and mind through all the steps described previously, then you are clearing up your energy. The more your energy is cleared up, the more in tune with your natural rhythm you become. In tune with your rhythm, your vision can emerge. With vision, you have a reason to live through the low times and a motivation for getting out of bed, taking excellent care of yourself even when you don't want to, and the joy of bringing something beautiful in to the world. It's simple. I've had to disguise it in this book, but that's the juice right there. If you get it, then close the book, and go live your life. If you've forgotten, pick this book or another one up again and remember. Clear your energy, honor your rhythm, and live your vision. Wow, I like that one I'm going to steal that from myself and put it up on my wall, Clear your energy, honor your rhythm, live your vision.

We now resume our book …

Bipolar has a lot in common with water. When water flows from the mountains to the ocean, it rarely, if ever, goes in a straight line. Water has its own rhythm, and so does each of us. Your rhythm may not fit in into our culture's preconception. Does this make you wrong or broken?

Let me go a step further. Imagine that the water in the river is actually your life-force energy. Life events come along and try and straighten you out here and there. Avalanches, floods, trees falling. Things happen that restrict the flow of energy or redirect you from your natural rhythm. Over time, water will compensate and reestablish its own rhythm or eat away at what's blocking it until it's flowing where it wants to again just look at what's at the bottom of the Grand Canyon.

All the suggestions so far in this book have been about removing the blockages to your natural energy flow. The closer you are to your true energy, the better you are at finding your own rhythm. As long as you are able to not bring harm to yourself or others, and are able to provide food and shelter in your life, who cares if your rhythm doesn't follow a prescribed pattern?

The more I've tuned in to this, and accepted the fact (I'm a bit goofy at times and a bit moody at times), the less crazy I feel. That's a biggie; let me repeat that. The more I've accepted the fact that I'm a bit goofy at times, and a bit moody at times, the less crazy I feel. I've realized that when I try to fit into the rhythms around me instead of the rhythms in me, then I feel the craziest and act accordingly, and this mistake has gotten me into a lot of trouble.

The more I became aware of my body, mind, and spirit, and the natural flow within me, the better I was able to see the flows outside of myself and integrate with them to the best of my ability without compromising my internal integrity. This required that I let go of many inhibitions I had about being "normal." Fortunately, there are many sane people such as myself on this planet who see "normal" as ridiculous so if you find yourself surrounded by "normies," take heart you will soon attract one of us sane "crazies" into your life.

When your muddy water begins to clear, your soul can emerge, and your visions can begin to blossom …

Spirit
Introduction
I was a strange child and often asked uncomfortable questions to adults. In fact, one day at Sunday school, I asked my teachers (who I found out years later were actually deeply religious) this question: "All the good people go to heaven, right?" "Yes, George," they replied. "And all the bad people go to hell?" "Yes, George," they answered, hardly hiding the enthusiasm in their voice with these wonderful breakthroughs they were making with me. (I hardly ever showed up for church, much less Sunday school, and it was always under protest.) "Well … if the good people in heaven were truly good people, wouldn't they want to go to hell to help the bad people get to heaven?" "Umm, uhh, gee, well …" I never did get a straight answer from then on, and after I repeated this story to my folks, they said I didn't have to go to Sunday school anymore. I finally got to stay home alone on Sundays, and I attended what I used to call the Church of the Great Outdoors.

I tell you that story because I think it relates to the bipolar experience. We see heaven and hell on a regular basis. When we study spirituality, we learn ways of lifting and coping with our times in hell and being able to enjoy our times in heaven more usefully. More importantly, our mission in life can become to help those in hell see heaven again and be with them if they choose to turn to the light again.

As we begin to see the aspects of both heaven and hell

inside ourselves, we begin to recognize them in others. It becomes easier over time to determine a person's spiritual position, and it is a natural outcome to want to guide people back to light. Because our trail is so well traveled inside ourselves, we are pretty good at helping others discover the trail to a better spot in their lives. We aren't necessarily here on planet Earth in a human body to go from A to Z or from cradle to grave. We are here for the journey between heaven and hell. We aren't the good people in heaven going to hell to help bad people, and we aren't all bad either. We are intimately familiar with both places, and some of us choose to help others see new possibilities.

If I get an e-mail tomorrow from God that says he/she doesn't exist or has quit, then I'm outta here. Flat and simple. Spirituality is the foundation of my ability to exist and thrive all these years without meds. I've worked with other bipolar people who don't have a fundamental belief in a benevolent power greater than themselves, and, quite simply, what I have to offer doesn't work without that kind of belief. I believe that spirituality is such an individual, intimate experience with what I like to call one's creator, that there is no way I could assume to steer you in the right direction without a similar belief.

I firmly believe that God is like the sun, and the many different rays of light that emanate out from the center are the many different paths to God. Each of us is a ray of light, a golden thread. Sure, you can follow this path or that for a while to get a clue and develop a few theories or practices similar to your own. But, ultimately, your journey with God is up to you. So let me offer to you what I have discovered as a starting point or a chance to compare notes.

Help!

I was newly sober, my girlfriend and I were in the process of breaking up, and I was already in a low. The school year was ending, and I didn't have a lot of cash and didn't have a clue about summer plans. Bigger than that, I was tired. Felt useless. All this effort to create a better life, and I could watch it all fall apart and go away again. I didn't have a lot of tricks in my bag yet, but I remembered one.

Help! The shortest, most effective prayer in the business. I felt lost and hopeless and concerned that I would soon be contemplating taking my own life again every day, which I hadn't done in long time. I had been living in a miracle with lots of positive changes internally and externally, yet somehow it felt like all was about to be lost. I don't know where it was that I came to this conclusion, but I know it was near a dirty bathroom, because that is where I went. Got in a stall, got on my knees, and asked for help.

There were no bolts of lightning or sudden cures for cancer popping into my brain, but someone pissed me off the next day at a support meeting. Turns out he thought I was invading his turf. He was one of the youngest like I was and liked the extra attention. I had no clue, yet I thought this guy was a jerk, until he offered to give me a ride home after the meeting. It took a few more tries, and before long, two twenty year olds were terrorizing the town like two-year-olds. Super Soakers, arcades, movies.

We were a menace to society in every fun way possible. Not to mention we both had an affinity for video games, staying up late, and watching movies. It was a great friendship that couldn't have happened at a better time. I didn't know what I needed; I just knew I needed help. Help came in the form of a new best friend. Charles, if you ever read this, let me know what you think of Xbox vs. PlayStation.

Prayer can be as complicated and formal as we like. I've found it works best when I'm really ready to receive. Sincerity seems to be born in desperation. The swings of bipolar and isolation can breed emptiness and willingness to try a new way. Our depths can eliminate all memory of good and what has worked in the past, yet our lows also can open us up to new techniques because we need them so desperately.

This buildup of our toolbox of ideas comes out when we are working with someone else in a dark space. A technique or insight from prayer may only work once or twice for us, yet our need to receive and our willingness to receive opens us up to be a storehouse of ideas for helping others to recover. This is one of the gifts of the down cycle, when we are truly ready to turn it around; we can receive so much, and, in turn, can serve others that much more effectively.

Daily
It was a hot, muggy August morning at a loading ramp

in the concrete jungle of Seattle's freight yards. My dad, with newly acquired trifocals, greying hair (which I had helped with, he claims), was giving me a refresher on how to make sailors blush with his verbal repertoire. His current hat was pitched like a weather vane to broadcast his mood. It was straight forward, and his lower jaw was clenched not a good sign for mere mortals.

We were in the process of moving household goods from Brooklyn to Vancouver Island, because my grandfolks, now in a rest home, no longer needed them. I'd been on my "path" for about three years and had reached the "Jesus" year, with only twenty-three revolutions around the sun. Everything was beautiful and spiritual, including me, no matter what. I was ten feet tall, bulletproof, and a legend in my own mind, when it came to not getting upset, even in the face of my father's current tirade.

My habit at the time was to carry spiritual literature in my back pocket. I had a subscription from a church with a positive mental focus and had found it quite helpful to always have a booklet with me. I would pull it out from time to time if I felt stressed, anxious, or bored, which was a lot that day. Soon, I would regain my composure and continue on.

About a day and a half into this fiasco, observing none of my usual reactions to his behavior, (at least on the surface), my father asked me what the hell I was reading. I told him. He grunted, which indicated to me he wanted me to read it to him. I did.

Divine synchronicity was abundant that day; I read the perfect words to soothe an otherwise @#$@#$ moment. "Humph!" was his reply. An hour or so later, and a few more classic screw-ups with frazzled shipping clerks, we found ourselves quietly reading another passage. Right on cue, it fit the moment perfectly, probably something about patience or divine timing.

The rest of the trip followed the same pattern. We dealt with rental trucks, ferries, border guards, traffic, and relatives, not to mention having to carefully move family heirlooms. At the end of that trip, I gave my father the booklet and got another. Life moved on. I got busy, very busy, and needless to say, my Jesus phase passed, and soon I was doing my part to carry on the family tradition of helping sailors blush.

Fifteen years later, my father shows up one day, listens to me go off for about five minutes, and I watch him quietly pull a pamphlet out of his back pocket. Yep, he'd gotten his own subscription and had carried one in his back pocket ever since. It was because of him that day that I didn't quit my job. Thanks, Dad.

Gratitude
I was in a dark time, living in a trailer again, hating life, and sitting on the human recyclables depository. That morning, I had read some positive, mushy stuff, and this one had said something strange. It said to thank God for the negative things in your life because they are teaching you the way to greater good. Humph. That was stupid. I contemplated this for a while and realized my day

couldn't possible get any worse, even though nothing big was happening, which was part of the problem.

I started grudgingly thanking God for every menial, stupid, and inane thing that had happened to me and in me that day. Every little thing. Every little inch in the storm. I said, *Okay, all you little gurus (teachers), teach me your good*. I don't remember what they were or what they taught me. I just know I felt better. The next day, as soon as negatives showed up, I thanked them on the spot. Lo and behold, before the day was out, I started seeing seemingly bad things as good, before I took them in as negative in my mind. Wow.

Not long after, I realized I was not living in any kind of dream I cared about, and I decided to move on with my life, so I did. I see that inglorious moment on the throne in my bathroom as the spark that triggered a whole new, positive direction in my life. Gratitude it's not just for the obvious good in your life. Remember to thank your little teachers (problems) as well.

Breathe on the Inside
I was on vacation in Hawaii, the first in over five years of hard work and a recent divorce. There was plenty of money in the bank, a jeep, sunny skies, and no worries, yet I was hating life and myself. It stunned me at first. *Why could I possibly be having a bad day on a day like today?*

I had to take a moment to realize that I hadn't had much time for bad internal days in a long time. I was on vacation, and it didn't matter. Sure, I would rather be my happy-go-lucky self the entire time, yet maybe there were other parts of me that I had pushed away for so long that they needed some sun and fun too.

It took awhile for this to settle in, and meanwhile I found as many little muddy roads as I could to explore. I must admit I thrashed that jeep it was fun. When I was ready to look inside again, I realized the inner wisdom was right: maybe I did not need to force myself to be happy when all I really wanted to do was let my inner emotions breathe and maybe even heal a bit. The more I finally accepted this, the more I was able to calm down a bit and enjoy my days in a bit more silence than usual. Toward the end of my time there, I was also a bit more at peace inside.

Tuning into and finding your internal spiritual space is important. You may not like what you see at first, yet it could cause a lot of extra stress if you ignore it. It may not be convenient to "feel" it right now, yet now may be the best opportunity.

Years earlier, I had been sitting in my car when I had a premonition to get out of the car and walk immediately. I ignored it and ended up cracking the windshield with my fist. I had just told my story for the first time to a friend. I'd put it off for months, but he seemed interested, so I opened up and shared what had happened at sixteen before I moved out on my own.

All the craziness and unresolved turmoil boiled up. I had tried every sane approach I could, to create a better living space for myself to finish high school in, yet I'd met stone walls everywhere and had ended up running away before finally getting a trailer to live in and a job to support myself with while I finished high school.

I hadn't been aware of how locked up I was inside or even aware that I had an inside yet. This led to cracking my windshield, yet fortunately not my fist (the karate classes must have been working, too bad I chose my car as an opponent). If I had followed my intuition, I could have prevented damage to my car, and released the energy through walking instead of scaring my friend and pissing myself off more with the damage I caused. I ended up letting my friend take my car and I walked most of the way home to cool my head a bit. In the long run it was a very valuable lesson learned.

With bipolar, there is a constant dance of awareness needed between our internal states and external events, both in the moment and in the near future. We are completely manual on this one. Our autopilot doesn't regulate transitions on its own. The more we see where we are inside, and look at what is coming up and how it's going to affect us, the better we can regulate. For instance, say I'm in a really good space internally, but I've got some uncomfortable events coming up. I take a moment to judge, *Am I stable enough now to make it through, or do I need to line up some extra support? Am I ready to do this now, or should I reschedule?* If I'm in a good enough space, it shouldn't be that big of a deal, and I can get through it.

Finding Gratitude in Bipolar

Homework/Lifework assignment: I invite you to meditate for hours in the back of your mind, going through your day, walking your dog, washing dishes. Ask your self the question; *What is the good of my current mental state, up down and in between?* Find something, no matter how seemingly small, to be grateful for in it. This is a liberating exercise, which leads to thriving.

If you take one item only from this book, take this one. It is the single most transformative thought, which all other gifts can spring from. Gratitude. Thank your higher self for creating and allowing this experience that you are in right now. Find reasons your current challenges are serving your long-term visions. Look, and look hard; your happiness depends on it.

Rat Race

I used to think, *If only I could stop the rat race and be a monk, how easy life would be.* Have you ever tried it? I was a quasi-unofficial wannabe monk for about three years (I volunteered as a cook and groundskeeper in a couple spiritual communities). Can you possibly imagine turning off your TV, cell phone, radio, MP3 player, etc. Take away all your distractions and live and work simply and quietly. Try it, and you might like it.

When we let go of all the busy-ness in our lives and invite the quietness, any unresolved shadows have a tendency to surface. I know this firsthand. Those are the scariest times I've ever had. Once I had worked through the current batch of shadows, it was also the most peaceful I've ever been. I was quite content to continue living that way, but God had other plans, and if there is one thing the lumps on my head have taught me, it's better to listen and follow the gentle whispers from the still-small voice inside, than to wait for the 2×4s to show up.

Part Three
A Guided Tour (Up, Down, and Back to Normal)

Introduction
At this point in the book, I have redefined the definition of bipolar, and looked at why and how you can positively affect your body, mind, and spirit. Now we look beyond. "What if I do all these things and I still have swings?" Good question. Sorry, no insta-fixes, no pills. No magic spells. What I have to offer takes willingness, tenacity, and patience for gradual improvement over time. There is a component of learning how to take care of ourselves to smooth out the ride, there is also an element of perspective, in learning to appreciate the value of the ride. This is why I've included this section. It is a guided tour of going up, going down, and finding the middle ground again. I used to call it, "NOW WHAT????".

I've found there are as many ways to go up as there are forms of bipolar. Fortunately for me, my bipolar is not limited to one particular way of getting high. I experience a full range from slow creeping highs to instantaneous highs. It's important to remember that "high" can imply happy, which at times it is; however, a high can also be extremely uncomfortable and compulsively dangerous if you are an untreated bipolar person.

Going Up
Homicidal
I have seen the inside of murder. Her name was Kari. She wasn't the first woman I ever fell in love with, but she was the most intense love experience I had ever felt. We had come close through talks, but never physically. The line inside me between friendship and sex was blurry and

raging.

When I was relatively new on the spiritual journey, my hormones were the primary regulator of my bipolar. Kari went away with another male friend of hers for the weekend. Murder wasn't part of my plan for life. I'd already been locked up once. No way in hell was I going to be locked up again. All weekend I had the wiggers.

I call it the wiggers, because the vision is continuous and wants to destroy everything. I get caught between two shows on the same channel of a TV. A flash of reality, a flash of delusion: one seductive, one grasping. My hands shake, and my mind races.

That weekend it didn't matter how fast I rode my bicycle or how many miles I walked. Jumping in my car, finding the guy, and killing was all I wanted to do. It wasn't just a passing thought of rage; it was a vision I lived inside of for three days. Ninety percent of me saw blood. Ten percent of me screamed to do everything but get in the car. I teetered all weekend. It became obvious to me how easily I could slip into the impending lure of resolving my visions without thought of consequences.

A path without medication is treacherous at times. I share this story in order for you to get the full picture and to help you decide your path. I am not a participant in the medication lifestyle; I am a pioneer of the raw bipolar experience. I've heard that, with medication, moments like this can be avoided.

After reading this, think about it. What is best for you and the life you choose to live? Is the pure, unmediated bipolar lifestyle really for you, or do you have other goals that need not be interrupted? I always have, and always will, give myself the choice of going on meds if I get to a point where I've had enough. Until that day, I get by the lows and crazies and enjoy the greater bipolar opportunity. Please choose wisely your life may depend on it.

Warning: Do Not Try This Alone!
I get through a wigger moment as best I can, call in sick, go to the bathroom, or bolt the scene, if necessary. Then I get to my bed, couch, or car, and wrap myself up as best I can, while rocking back and forth. Ideally, I call or ask for help, and most times I am able to, and someone is available; otherwise, I've found that non-action and distraction work as a first aid measure until better help is available. I have a comfortable couch and a lot of DVDs. I know where the theaters are and my favorite restaurants. I travel with a dedicated credit card for a hotel room and the ability to create safety.

When you are in a high crisis mode, it's time to choose the lesser of evils. A stuffed belly will pass, and a couple hours numbing out on the couch won't get you locked up. It is not a long-term solution; yes, I've tried that too. To keep eating leads to a big belly, and distraction in any compulsive form spins me into a long-term victim cycle. It's not fun. Getting in touch with a friend or counselor as soon as possible is the next step back to reality. I have experienced the wiggers from time to time, and I have successfully pulled through. Help from other humans who understand is the key to success.

I never could comprehend how anyone could kill someone. After that weekend, I knew I was just as capable as any convicted murderer. I saw the inside of murder, and it became my example of unhealthy visions and untreated bipolar highs. It was my wake-up call to be guided by spirit and truth, rather than unguided emotion. Knowing I could easily kill, I began focusing my energy on the positive visions while I was high. The more I was able to create with them, the more I had to lose if tempted by a dark one. Using my high visions for positive outcomes became a regular lifestyle choice. I could better serve people with my positive visions, rather than hurt people with my unresolved fear and expectations.

Super Brain
I get so involved in a super brain high that I become indifferent to other people's realities. As you can see, up times are not always fun, for innocent bystanders …

Tell me it's impossible, and give me a screaming deadline, and super brain comes to life. There is a way; I am a will. My brain loves to wrap around impossible, complicated ideas. At first, I'm a bit slow and seemingly "stupid," as I repeat simple questions and get up to speed, and then all goes silent.

When I go silent on a project, watch out; I have just figured it out. I go from passive student helper, to Mr. Hotshot. Horns sprout out of my head, and I am ten feet tall and bulletproof. I'm finally back on the throne and can see everything. It annoys me that people are moving more slowly and can't keep up with what I'm telling them just because I don't fill in all the words.

I begin thinking so hard and fast from every angle that I don't bother __complete sentence or remember answers __what __asked. I'll ask the same simple questions over and over---I'll ask the same simple questions over and over, until the answers overcome the distractions inside me. If they would only trust me, I could tell them everything. I've got it figured out, and anything is possible. I see it.

WARNING!!!!
Excited? Everything is wonderful? Irritable? Moving faster? Missing words?

Decision Time
Can I have a happy time now? Can I enjoy this one, or do I have obligations? Either way, just like a pilot getting ready for takeoff, I need to run through a checklist. Is this a natural high, or is it being augmented by lack of food, sleep, water, emotions, etc.? Check in with someone, i.e., call the control tower. "Hey, guess what, I'm feeling really giddy and high right now, so would you mind keeping an eye on me?"

If the crazy train departs the station before I notice, I'm usually stomping on the gas. People are moving slowly, but I'm actually talking and moving faster. The little horns growing out of my head form sharp points;

I realize how stupid people are. Why don't they get it? Why can't they see all the possibilities I see?

There is a lot to do, and my brain starts going in a million different directions. Each thought or task is a new train departing from the station, and my brain starts riding each one and trying to complete the tasks simultaneously. I see possibilities and solve problems, yet often leave an even bigger uncompleted mess for the peons to clean up.

Stop. Breathe. (Note to Self)

If now is not a good time to enjoy a visionary state, I try to get grounded. I'll call a friend who is aware of my gifts, and ask for help. Help in getting to a park, exercise, water, meditation, massage, stomping feet, or jumping into the ocean are all healthy things I can do to find Earth again. Then I'll look at my current schedule and plan a fun activity. Just like with our lows, we can choose to delay our highs with practice more on this in a minute.

As a visionary, I can be inside the blueprint of a project. When I get something, I'm not kidding. I can visualize being an electron underneath a control button at the Arctic Ocean and watch myself travel the 24-gauge wires 800 miles to the pumps that load the tankers with crude oil. Just like in dreams, I can live inside work projects. This ability is excellent for troubleshooting and seeing where problems are.

When I'm balanced and on a functional high, it's beautiful. When my ego gets involved, it's ugly. I'll wake up the next day with a mental hangover if I remember, or clueless to the wary stares from co-workers if I tuned it out. It is easy to sit and wallow in the shame. I have. I do my best to review the days when I have experienced an ugly high. The conclusion is usually the same. Bad highs are preceded by days of no routine in the morning to get my head and heart right. It's great to have a super computer brain, if used compassionately. It's obnoxious to be around if the human has left.

The Inside of *Huh?*
There is a *huh* period of time before super brain shows up. Stay with me on this one. Remember the last time your senses, all of them, were completely blown away by a gourmet meal? Was it big enough to create a moment of *huh?* A pause in which the brain is catching up with all that it has just received. Input overload. It's when the mouse on your computer decides to take a coffee break and just sit while you wiggle it. Imagine, if you would, that every project, day, new idea, concept, lesson, person, place, etc., was an overwhelming sensory cathedral. This, of course, has a simple solution. It is sensory overload, so give the patient a drug and just slow him down. Hmmm. How sure are we about this? What if it's just a pause of *huh?* What if a moment is created or given to catch up? What if some of us are designed to take in all the senses, and once we have taken in a concept or experience long enough, then we can live, move, shape, form, and create inside of it, which is where the speed comes from?

Did that last paragraph make any sense to you? If it did, I like the way you think, so come create with me. If not, here may be why. It did not follow a "normal" structure. It started out with one idea (a moment of *huh*), evolved into a question (Have you ever experienced a sensory cathedral overload?), answer (put people on drugs), opinion (good idea? *not*), solution (Create or allow moments to catch up and get inside new sensations), conclusion and description (we are overwhelmed, go slow, catch up, then go create really fast); this is a super brain in action. Breathe. Now read these two paragraphs ten times in a row, ten times as fast, and think harder than you have thought in your entire life. Welcome to our world. If you feel slow and confused afterward for a little bit before the light bulb comes on, then you can understand our huh? moments.

Houston, We Have a Probl -click
I used to play red light/green light with my life all the time. Green light, crisis mode, go, go, go, and who cares about food, sleep, and shelter? Red light, shut down, no think, zone out, who cares?

After years of taking really good care of myself, I recently slipped into it again. I let the undisciplined crisis mode out of the cage and performed very well.

I'm not aware of when my identity or daily routine were lost. I vaguely remember at some point wondering when was the last time I had showered or smelled clean clothes. I felt like I could go, go, go forever, even after the crisis was over. I was a completely different person, like I had been years ago. This mode of operation was normal again for the moment, an eerie glimpse into my crazy past. I did not want to snap out of it. It took about three days of gently re-introducing a daily routine before I felt like my fangs and horns had retracted, and my cape could fit back inside the phone booth.

It's nice to know that I can still fit into the red and blue suit with a big red "S" on the front, but losing contact with normality and the ability to know who I am or what gentle progress I was making on my next goals, was scary. It was a window back into the way I used to unconsciously live with bipolar before I seized it as an opportunity. Thank God for books like this that teach us about stability and the middle ground.

It all started when my morning solitaire game at work was interrupted by my best friend. He had the audacity to show up and expect me to get something done. His paychecks were signed by a different company, and he actually had to work, poor guy. My job is more like being a Maytag repair man waiting for something to break before the cattle prod in my chair gets me up to go fix it or guys like him with projects show up. It was a major network cutover. I am good at networks. The more screwed up and complicated, the better.

We were lulled into a lullaby of our own making when the first three stations went smoothly. Assuming we had once again proven our prowess over the digital voice world, we moved on to a simple software upgrade. Somewhere between 4.5 v1.1. and XPL, oh, good grief, my brain went into active standby. This wasn't my specialty anymore, and he seemed to be slugging away at the digital dragons just fine. I was the responsible party, so I couldn't leave. This would have been a manageable situation for my bipolar brain, a simple maintenance mode activity level.

Enter stage left, the electricians. They needed to shut off power to the computers and the phones. Normally, I would have told them to take a flying @@#, but I failed to convince the head shed engineers that unscheduled outages on sensitive communication computers miles from the nearest electronic parts stores were not a good idea. Some of our equipment requires a silent prayer and holding your tongue just right when you turn it off and on, hoping that all the electrons decide to behave when you give them electricity again.

We shut down the power. Then the big one hit. Back in town (400 miles away), the main server takes a power hit and decides not to get up again. Joe used to say, when it comes to communications techs, you can talk about us, but you can't talk without us. People were talking, but they weren't' talking on the phones or sending each other e-mails. Miles from nowhere in the peak of construction season, it's a big deal.

It took three days before systems starting coming back online, and things began to resemble normal again. Three days after that, I was back to playing solitaire and had had my fix of red light/green light for a while. What's just as important as getting into a high is being able to pick up the pieces afterward and reestablish normal. Yes, highs can be fun if major damage hasn't occurred, but middle ground can be much more productive and satisfying in your life.

Happy Highs
Defining the line between what is a healthy high and at what point the line has been crossed is the art form of being consciously bipolar. It is an active art that is practiced daily. On the inside, I have extreme compassion for all forms of addiction and compulsion. Each time a natural high comes my way, without any pill or activity stimulating it, I have a choice. At times, I've been the junkie and enjoyed the ride, hoping I don't wreck or get in trouble, and at times I've chosen to take actions toward calming down and seeking balance.

Going Down
Empathy Cycle
Suddenly
My grandfather passed (the one that made up stories for me while I looked at the pictures), when I was about 7. I only spent part of the first two years of my life with him, but I remember him as a good buddy and friend. It sunk in that he was gone, and I would never hang out with him again. Emptiness.

My uncle died when I was 11. He was really cool, he flew his own plane and we had ice cream eating contests, which I'm still convinced I may have given him a run for his money more then once. I know my belly used to ache a lot when we called it truce. I was completely devastated. Lost. Gone. Bye, Bye. I knew him, I liked him, and each time he visited was special. I liked how aware and alive his eyes were.

They were gone.

Grief and sensitivity to loss is the only way I know how to explain the sudden empathy cycle of bipolar. Here is the kicker; there isn't always an event or defining moment that can trigger the cycle.

Here is the weird part. It's a sunny day, time off from work, fun things lined up to do, and next thing I know I'm curled up on my couch in a dark cave drooling. Gone.

It's taken a lot of time for me to sort this one out. Here is what I've discovered so far; moments that overcome me like this require compassion, and patience. If I'm at work or unable to curl up and properly feel and process it, I HAVE TO, make an appointment with myself to feel it at the first opportunity.

When I have taken the time to ask spirit to guide me, what's going on what do I need to feel hear say see? Then if I'm quiet and patient a little longer, I'm usually shown. A friend in need, a part of me bubbled up ready to heal from my past, or practical things at work that need to go in a different direction, or someone or some thing needs a voice to speak for them or encourage them to speak.

It's kind of creepy at times because it is why I think bipolar and shamanism are linked. It's kind of like something comes over us, we go into our huts or caves, we groan, mutter, roll around until we see and say what needs to be said.

There are times when I have honored this process, and there are times when I have ignored, stuffed, run screaming into the dark night away from this process. Each time I have surrendered to the process, a greater good in my life or others has occurred. Each time I have avoided it there is usually loss or missed opportunity, which at times has lead to greater harm.

Gradually
Gradually going down can be the same as suddenly, but stretched out over time with a few added stages. I have found a spiritual focus to be beneficial, it is not something we have a whole lot of space for in our culture; but we could.

The spiritual side of going down slowly can start out with self-analysis and self-judgment. It can slip in silently to our day in the back of our minds and can be harsh and dangerous, until we become conscious of it. Then, if we can turn it into compassion and acceptance, we can tune in to the next layer. Flipping the negatives about me has taken a lot of reading, prayer, writing, and time. I used to listen to the judgments of me about me, accept it, and keep listening to it as I continued on with my crappy day.

One day I decided to set up court in my head. I decided primary judgments about me occurred with information I had at the time in the past. Maybe they were no longer valid and I was worthy of a retrial. So each case brought up by the negative me about me, I appointed to the new me representing myself as judge and jury. I would listen to the evidence presented, study, read, write, and come up with a new ruling. Sometimes I would agree, and let it stand for a later trial. Sometimes I would throw it out of court.

Overtime, if the pesky negative side of me about me brings up the same case again, I can refer him to the previous positive ruling give him hug and thank him for his concern. I have to ask without Mr. Negative me about me, would I be as sensitive and honest in my interactions with others and myself? So yes I thank Mr. Negative for being thorough with my past and present behaviors, so that I can see myself for who I currently am more clearly, accept myself as I am, and see areas I would like to improve.

The important thing is to see/catch negative self-analysis, and judgment quickly because there is usually always, a deeper level.

A bipolar person is going to feel IT. Whatever IT is, it is not an option. You are going to feel it, whether it is the universal pain of what is going on with the planet or the first flower in spring.

In the back of your mind, a dialogue can be going: *What is it? Spirit guide me what is it*
I need to see? What am I not seeing? What am I not feeling?

When we get to that gift, that gem, we can record it, we can write it out, or we can call someone and share it. Nine times out of ten, that is the trigger; that is the piece that is going to lead us back out. We can grab a hold of it, and be lifted, and led to a whole new vision.

We might tune in to someone who needs a call. I've come out of the empathy phase before and called someone who says, "I'm so glad you called. I was really having a hard time or thinking about suicide." I wouldn't have known about this if I hadn't tuned in and felt what was going on.

We need people who are able to do this more often. I'm willing to bet that, the more comfortable we become with the empathy cycle, the more we will be able to tune in to others in need and help prevent tragedies as well as provide comfort to those in need. Too often, we isolate when we are negative. Have you ever had a good friend call out of the blue when you were down? Isn't it the greatest feeling to be loved in that way? It's kind of ironic, but I've experienced it too many times to doubt that there is truth to our empathy cycles being connected with others in need.

It's not always about you or your past or what you have or have not done. Sometimes it is simply a distress call from someone you know that doesn't go through the current communication channels we are comfortable with.

I Felt So Much Better Once I Gave up Hope …
If the empathy persists long enough, your defenses break

down and, consciously or not, you are going to ask the question,

Why?

Let me share with you my wisdom, friend. We do what we can do. We can take the best possible care of ourselves, but for some reason we end up, as my father used to say, looking up out of the gutter at the rear end of a worm.

The most startling reply I've ever heard from spirit is, *Why not you?* After years of anguish, trying to figure out what I did wrong, I've realized that I feel better a lot more quickly when I give up trying to figure out why I had to. Because I would be so upset at myself when I questioned, *Why am I this way again?* It could be food, it could be a thought, it could be an emotional event, it could be a counseling event, it could be how I perceived that someone treated me, but I really did not know for sure.

What I focus on is where I end up. If I keep thinking about all the things I've done wrong, it's like picking up an ugly stick and beating myself over the head. When I put on my rose-colored glasses, I can see the good things. Did I eat? Do I have a place to sleep? Am I under restraints or in lockup, or do I still have my freedom?

Sometimes I can get myself to go for walks, and each step becomes a mantra, I say or think, "positive, mental attitude." Over and over again, each step, positive mental attitude. I do this when I can't think of anything positive, and I'm trying to block out negative thoughts. Eventually, the energy shifts, or I might finally find something positive to focus on. Often, if I can just find a spark, it's enough to find another positive. Many depressions or empathies have been reversed by this one simple technique.

Make Love to Your Depression
Something happens. Okay, over time, when we get to know ourselves a little better, we can know when an event or energy is coming that may not be easily diverted. Breakups, deaths, jobs, project completions everyone's triggers are different.

Make a date. Put on some music, comfortable chair, nice dinner (it's a great time to take yourself out to dinner), come home, light a candle. You can even put on a sad movie. And I just have at it. Cry, feel, stare whatever you need to do. Be warm and comfortable, and call a friend, if possible, to get support.

It's amazing. When I've consciously participated in my depression, I've usually learned something about myself, which leads to not being as affected or triggered in the future. I have also gotten over it much sooner. I am a master at avoiding stuff. Nope, sorry I already have the corner on the market. Yet, when I've honored my energy and feelings, from a positive perspective, they aren't always as hairy scary as my mind likes to think they are. This is the key.

The mind doesn't like big emotions and low energy, because it's not in control for a moment or two. If we are not under major obligations, our minds don't need to be in total control. What's wrong with relaxing your mind as well as your emotions? When you let your sensitivities catch up and process all that you have received recently, you are able to experience your sensitivity openly again.

This leads into pace of life. When obligations or internal pressures have dictated that I march on, no matter what, then brick walls are not far off. Maintaining the ability to receive and let go of sensitivities and emotions is vital to living with bipolar. Real or imagined avoided sensitivities can build up a depression sooner than anything else.

Processing our sensitivities is not always comfortable, fun, or seemingly necessary. High speed on demand processing of our sensitivities and perceptions is a feature in the autopilot of our minds that is not always functional, and can easily be overwhelmed and shut down completely. I don't know how "normal" people process all the information they receive throughout a day. I suspect they don't receive as much and are better able to let go of what they do receive. In this case, ignorance is bliss.

The good in this is if we treat our antennas with care, they also create the finer details in our dreams. These same antennas, which can be a nuisance to take care of in daily life, are subtle touches we use to interact with someone who is depressed or to see and affirm the vision of others when they are high. These antennas are a big part of the bipolar experience that I've heard gets numbed through medication; fortunately, I've never had to and never intend to experience this loss.

Suicide or Phoenix Rising?
I call this the Phoenix rising experience. We see this as the illusion of suicide. We burn down to the ashes and blow away. Some part of your life, some part of the way you are being, something is not right, and it is not that you want to shoot yourself; instead, you want just some part of your self to die, to go away. You are done with that part, and you want to let it go. Out of these ashes, your new life and your new truth are born. Here is how it happened for me.

Winter is a lonely time in the park. The wooden two-by-six observation posts for the bird migrations are empty. It's cold in the slight wind. Feet crunch on the crisp snow. My mind is in its usual state lately: gone. Checked out, left the scene, life sucks, who gives a shit anyways? The usual topic of late creeps back in. Yeah, let's do it it's time. Car wreck? Gun? Break a hole in the ice and jump in? Where is the nearest cliff?

I find myself standing on the platform, looking out over the field, a few blades of straw still stubbornly standing. The field is kind of like me, because 90 percent of me wants to die right now, 10 percent keeps going, one foot in front of the other, and I don't know why anymore. I look down, and I wonder if it's far enough to break my neck and will it hurt? Wasn't it just yesterday that I was happy, conquering the world? I hate this disease. Rope, I could get a rope and hang myself right here. Fuck it, this is a perfect spot. I think I have one in my car.

Back at my place, I'm hungry, so I nuke something and shove it into my mouth and drown it with a pint of ice cream. The thoughts never leave my mind: I know how to tie the knot, and it's only a short walk away. A couple movies later, I'm still awake, going over and over again in my mind exactly how I would do it. Slowly, my eyes close, and dreamland takes over …

I hang myself and watch my body swing, then become still and stiff. I see people discover my body, and soon there is a quiet service. My sisters and my folks show up, and that's about it. I feel better, completely dead at last. It's a quiet peace.

Finally, in my sleep, my mind is able to move on, and I start thinking about my day. I start to see something, and I wake up. I start writing furiously. I was fine yesterday and suicidal again today. Why? I woke up grouchy. I woke up extremely sensitive, and I had to deal with the damn world anyway. It's like all my senses were on high, and I could not get a break.

I wonder if that is why I ended up so dark. Hmm. What if I were to give myself a break on supersensitive days? A quiet lunch with myself, instead of hanging out with the guys. Or better yet, no shopping in busy stores that day.

The night goes on, and I see more of my extreme sensitivity and my need to create space for it. Toward morning, I've realized that these insights happened after

I died in my dream and woke up again. Maybe what died was my own insensitivity to how aware and overloaded I am some days. What if I could take better care of myself on certain days and avoid this particular suicidal trigger? Hmm, I'll have to try this.

I know this is controversial and scary, but I've had success with it numerous times and have reaped the benefits. The trick is to establish physical safety and allow the suicidal thoughts to be okay. This is never to be done alone. Period. Don't even kid yourself. Yes, losing your street clothes and underwear is a nuisance, but if that is only way you can create safety for yourself by being locked up then please do so.

If I am completely done with an untruth in my life and willing to feel and see the depth of the pain it is causing me, then I can begin to accept the need to let go and move on. It's not me wanting to kill myself; it is an unhealthy part of me wanting to let go.

I've been in this dark spot numerous times. I've seen it coming, taken care of myself, and let it wash through me. The next morning is always amazing, usually bringing a whole new perspective on life. It's a relief to be alive with new insights, a new strength, and renewal.

It is a knothole that I go through. I can go through the experience and wake up the next day and be so excited that there is sun, and there is green grass, and I am alive. The basic gift of being alive is that much sweeter after months of not wanting it, then suddenly seeing how beautiful it really is.

Truly dark times can take months even years to slip into. I'll do everything I can to stay on the sunny side, but at some point my rhythm is down. This is going to sound weird, but I think I've prolonged downers by avoiding and not facing them. Yet, when I've finally accepted that my soul is in a dark cave and needs retrieval, I can go into the dark side with an open mind, knowing it won't last forever, and chances are there is a gift in the back of the cave for me. Not always, but sometimes I get stuck and have to strictly adhere to a daily routine to get myself back out again. It's an art form, not a science, yet. Like I've said, this is an extremely advanced technique, and I am concerned about putting it out there. But my technique does need to be mentioned, because suicidal depression is the great fear surrounding bipolar, and maybe we could begin taking a more open-minded approach to it.

"Normal"
The normal phase is when the autopilot of the brain is functioning. Normal feels normal. We often don't know that we are normal. We blend in, and can forget the extreme highs and lows even existed. We can cruise along, if things are going well in our lives, months or even years can go by.

Normal can also just be a brief momentary pause or a window between phases. This can be very baffling to the witnesses of our strange behaviors as well as to ourselves, when we don't remember what happened, and others are giving us curious looks or are negotiating wide berths around us. If you know someone who is bipolar, it can be very supportive to gently touch base with that person and see if he or she even knows what happened. This can lead to you being a safe person to go to and check in with and to receive feedback from and encouragement, to help us steer around crisis modes and swings that may be avertable.

Either way, there are things we can do. The biggest is to breathe, relax, and be grateful, especially if we are lucky enough that we are aware of feeling normal. I remember that the first times I felt normal were amazing because, at first, I was thinking that something was wrong with me, something was different, and I couldn't figure out what it was. So I reviewed what was going on. When I got to the bottom of the list and figured that everything checked out okay, then I had a eureka moment: I was feeling *normal.*

The best thing we can do while feeling normal is to get back to or maintain our regular routine. It is a time when we can make progress by using our brains while they are "online." We can organize, clean, get supplies, plan ahead for trips and retreats, pay bills, and get caught up on paperwork.
I've found the best use of my time is to break down every task to the smallest complete steps and do my best to stick to one at a time. That way, if life or another mental event interrupts me, I don't have fifty incomplete things started and a big mess to deal with later. Instead, I may only have one or two things left undone. Taking complete steps is much easier for coming back up to speed when

my brain is next available for clear thought.

Sometimes, the best thing I can do while feeling normal is to curl up in a ball and read a book. Mental rest is okay and important. It may not be the biggest priority in my life right now, but it could be the most important.

If you feel normal for a longer period of time, your daily routine is really important to maintain, (1) as a good habit you don't want to lose, (2) because of the benefits from ongoing spiritual insight and growth, or (3) if you are going to need it again when you find yourself, high or low, triggered by a life event. Once you are in a high or low, it's much more difficult to begin again a routine than it is to maintain one while you are normal and transitioning into another phase. Maintaining a good routine can also prolong a "normal" period.

The Gentle Life
I've found, over time, the pace of my life slowing down. I'm not a mover and a shaker anymore. I don't need to be. I move and shake plenty on the inside, just sitting still. Because we have highs, lows, compassion for people, and a constant intake of information, whether it is from the people we interact with or from intuitions, it takes time to filter and integrate.

When we let go of busy-ness, and make time for "emptiness," we can fill it with necessary reflection and the processing of all the inputs available to us. We may not move or shake the world, but we might have an eye on what's truly important. Noticing a key event in another person's life, we may be more tuned in and supportive. Observing a not-so-swift move by our company, and we may have more focused energy to explain the errors in a way movers and shakers may be more receptive to.

There are daily-coffee-drinking movers and shakers who keep the world spinning. There are some of us that pay more attention to where the world is going and at what point, what junctures, is our energy most efficient in shifting a direction. Balanced, supported, bipolar people are good at this. If we are able to mellow out enough to process all that is going on, we can contribute to positive balanced directions.

An Aborted Launch
It was a lazy afternoon in May. I had a long five-hour drive up past the Yukon to a remote worksite; I was feeling mellow, and my friend Mac was coming along. It was a ten-hour drive for two hours work, all on overtime; we liked to call those bank runs easy money.

I was thinking about which engagement ring would look best on my sweetie's finger, knowing all the hours I worked this weekend would go toward buying one for her. It was all I could think about, being able to gaze into her eyes again soon. Her eyes that had never accepted the dramas I could create between my ears. Dramas and b.s., she would whisk away with her love and help me see that I really was a good guy. I was with a gorgeous woman who totally excited me, and she loved me back. No darkness I coughed up was going to change her mind. Thank God. Inside, I was in a state of bliss, while cranking out the work till I could fly out to see her again.

A co-worker asked me to stop by and help out a new hire with his timesheet before I hit the road. I soon made a mistake. I asked at what rate they had hired him on. Tech3. I could hear the steam coming up the pipes long before it shouted out my mouth. I was pissed and instantly in launch mode. Off guard, defenses taking a rest, my inner control center on idle, my insides were violently overtaken by a storm, and a freight train was moving up my chest. I hated shit like this. I could already feel that I was relegated to the observer seat, and I didn't like not knowing where this ride was going to end up.

The opening words I watched flow out of my mouth were "that's fucking bullshit." There was no yoga, no cup of tea, and no pause button. My helicopter ride was in an instant storm, and I was in the passenger seat again. My inner mind went through another grasp at the controls, knowing it was already hopeless. I watched an all-too-familiar tirade flow out of my mouth. I watched my co-worker roll his eyes in boredom and give the wide-eyed new guy the *ignore this quack* look. I hated it, but I couldn't stop. I knew my mind was going to spin into high gear, and it was going to be a long drive to the Yukon, before I was reasonable again.

Highs can be triggered this fast. Unresolved resentments are firewood waiting to torch off. I had known this for a while, yet thought I had it under control. Mistake number two was that I was temporarily off guard, being so deeply in love again. Not a mistake, but something to be aware of. Life events can cause us to be less wary of our mental states, especially if bliss or a feeling that "all is okay with the world" is part of the experience.

And this is why I loved her: my soon to be finance spoke up in my head, asking *How long are you going to be a victim this time?* I made another feeble attempt at the controls in my head, listening to her words, being pissed, and watching diesel flow into the tank of my vehicle.

Somehow, I had extracted myself from my co-workers office and found my way to the fuel depot to top off the tank. Back in the truck, driving to pick up my friend for the trip, her words started asking me why I was so pissed and what was my part in all of it. This time, I reached out for the control stick in my head and managed to scan a few of the gauges. Sure enough, low on food and water, but exercise was good. I had gotten up early that morning and swam, did yoga, and wrote.

I silently thanked God for what I had done that morning, as I pulled into a truck stop to get a bottle of water and a quick bite to eat. Without the routine that morning, right now could have been a lot worse. Many more miles would have spun by my brain before I did a spot check on the gauges.

As the food hit my stomach and cold water passed my lips, back on the road, I knew I was going to be okay, and I starting listening to her words, to what was really going on. This could have been a stormy restless night. Instead, loving words, a daily routine, and immediate positive actions averted the worst and got me back to the middle ground a lot sooner. Thank you, Kani, for the time you spent with me. We are no longer together, but I will never forget her loving words.

Part Four
The Symbiotic Opportunity

An Opportunity as Individuals
Initially, when some of my highs and lows had stabilized, and my life was heading in a really good direction, I didn't have bipolar symptoms for a while, almost as if bipolar had gone into remission. The sun kept coming up, and life moved on. Deeper issues kept coming to the surface. So, after a while, things got dark, and the heavy swings came back. This is when I really had to dig in with my newfound knowledge and belief in the positive power of the mind and spirit. Even though I had found a church with a positive attitude, some spiritual authors, and I had begun to learn things I could do in my daily life to help balance out my swings, I was down again, badly.

I started looking at what could possibly be good about being bipolar. After a long dark night of the soul, I found a few things. As I was recovering from a knee injury, I realized how much better care I took of myself when I was injured. I realized that my "brain" was in a way injured, and in order to feel normal and balanced, I had to have a daily routine, every day, even when I didn't want to.

This is a major reason why bipolar is a golden opportunity we are given each day we wake up: I can embrace the idea, *hey, guess what I'm bipolar, so what look at all the good things I can do right now to go in a positive direction today.* Each morning, we are given this choice. Some people wake up neutral or positive. So what. No matter how we wake up (research shows it is often moody or negative), we can choose to keep our lives going in a positive direction. It's so simple that it's easy to miss. If our minds were normal, we could go about our "normal" lives and never be aware of the greater possibilities we have access to.

If I was normal, I would still be working at a car wash in the town I grew up, or maybe I would have taken over my dad's business. Because I'm bipolar, trying to figure out how to fly this helicopter without autopilot, I've been on all kinds of adventures.

As I've learned how to fly, the landings are smoother (and more frequent for fueling), and the directions I fly are more conscious. I am living in dreams I once hoped were possible. Does it get easier? It's hard to say. Do I feel like a better pilot of my mind since I started? Hell, yes. I've got a lot more moves and choices than I ever imagined possible.

Nowadays, I don't go through the food store, worried if I have enough money for this week while hating my job, and carefully going over my budget. Now, I'm more concerned about getting my next treasure map updated, so I can keep expanding the universe I fly in. I believe this would have been impossible without the gift of the bipolar opportunity in my life. Have negative swings taken me through dark times? Yes. They have also led me through my worst fears, and when I got through to the other side, I was given extra ordinary skills to create what's next, without the fears I had just lived through.

Time and again, I've tested this theory. I feel good, the

stars are lined up, everything is going my way, with no highs lows or swings, and so I stop my daily routine. I might get by for a week, month, maybe even a couple months, depending on how well things were going. But, sooner or later, things fall apart, and life moves on. Here is the good news: I couldn't tell you how many times I've realized this, sat down, wrote it out, and began again.

Waking up gently, I shower, do yoga, read my daily spiritual books, write in my journal, and connect with and remind myself of the current dreams I'm working toward. Sure enough, no matter how low I've sunk or for how long, I start to feel better and eventually get excited about life again. It works; it really works. I don't recommend that you let it go as far as I have at times. There is no need to be as ornery as I am. Develop your own daily routine, and stick to it.

I am often impatient with the way I am or with the fact that I keep having swings, yet I've noticed it's not the big things I do every day that have the most effect on my life. It's been the little things. It's the little positive routines over time that have gently guided my life in positive directions and have led to the good times and the temporary remission of my bipolar symptoms. When times are good, and I've vigilantly maintained my daily routines no matter what, I've been able to stay in the good times longer instead of prematurely destroying them with swings I could have anticipated and been better able to ride out, instead of letting them crash on shore and disrupt my life.

Ultimately, my search for possible positive effects from bipolar is what led to the theories in this book. It is a message of hope and a description of the compassionate experience that goes along with our innate ability to dream and create a better reality, because of the way we are. We are not wired normally, thank God. We are wired with an ability to see and live in a better reality, if we choose, before it is materialized. This is why we are able to see and assist others with their dreams as well as our own and to help others in down times, because we are there and able to pull through. It's not easy, it takes daily work, but it is possible to work a good life with our special gifts instead of coping with a negative lifelong disease.

How We Can Help An Opportunity for Others
If you are getting ready to climb Mt. Everest or go into the Grand Canyon, are you just going to do it? There is a chance you'll want to hire an experienced guide. When a normal person is cruising along and he has a life event that triggers major mental swings, chances are there is going to be a bipolar person nearby. We can be right there with the person while he goes through a vision or a dark valley. If possible we walk beside the person gently, until he is able to negotiate his new life successfully.

That's what we do. That's the gift of being a bipolar person for others. We are going to feel it. We feel it on a regular basis. We go up, we go down, we go through the grief, and we go through the ecstasy and the vision. We are practiced at it. We are naturally drawn to helping others in times of need.

A bipolar person who is experienced with going up and down can be very supportive during this time. We are more likely to say, "Let's do it! Let's go climb Mt. Everest!" We see people's dreams and desires. We remember and affirm them. When the "normal" person is a member of our regular group, we check in with that person: *how are your dreams going?*

We know the emotional and energetic territory of the human experience. It is our natural role to help those who wander into the mental wilderness and need help with what they find or a way back to their daily lives. This is the beautiful symbiotic opportunity of a bipolar person. We do need help. We are strange people to hang out with. But we are a lot of fun, too, sometimes. And on the flip side, we can provide a lot of support. It is my belief that we are the original mental health counselors. We have been around since day one, and we are here to help.

Hope A Future
It may not be instant, but we can, through careful time and exercise of will in a positive direction, unwind the initial trauma and triggers of our erratic rhythms. Along the way, we can learn to see and not just cope with the bipolar experience but celebrate our sensitivity. Yes, we do appear to be crazy and to not make comfortable sense, and we are out of whack and see things from an entirely different angle.

I believe bipolar is curable. I believe it has a genetic

root, which is triggered by fight-or-flight trauma. Once the bipolar is triggered, the swings are going to keep occurring until the ancestral and current life trauma is dealt with, and one's truth and purpose in this life is discovered and lived.

I have once again created heaven in my current life. I was in a dark spot not that long ago and made the decision again to pick up my positive daily routine and start working toward my truth. I'm several years into this round, and I have created homeostasis with my life and truth. One of the pieces was picking up this book again and continuing to write out the truths I know about bipolar. One of the pieces was confronting the physical environment I was living in and overcoming my fear of letting go of comfort, in order to live where my mind, body, and spirit were called to live.

Another piece was consciously confronting my inner crap on a daily basis again. Turns out, there was a lot of grief I needed to feel, and now I'm into feeling anxiety and terror. And it is okay. After years of being on a "spiritual" path, I finally believe what many have been telling me, that I am beautiful and okay just the way I am, and so are my shadows.

This is the beauty and intensity of the bipolar experience, that we don't have the luxury of being numb to our truths and living a lie. If we are out of tune with where we belong and what we really need to be doing with our lives, we will be miserable. This curability is not instant. It takes a commitment to hope, larger than we imagined possible. It takes time relative to our willingness and ability to manifest the support we need.

Looking back, I can remember other times when my bipolar experience had gone into remission.
I was living my truth and in a loving community with support that accepted me as I am. Creativity was an active part of my life, and so was reaching in and helping others come out into their greater truth.

Lag time and lack of sustainability between understanding our next layers and truths are the threats to long-term remission from severe bipolar swings. I believe this can be lessened through awareness with books like this one, and a support network for positive, focused bipolar people.

We don't necessarily belong in the nine-to-five grind, or in formal roles. Much of our "work" is not seen on the physical plane, moving objects, whether they be paper or rocks, from one place to another. Our work is truth ours and that of those around us who are willing to see and work toward it.

Our need is love and acceptance. Our gift is to be able to see the deepest truths, that we are good and life is okay, and it can always get better if we listen and act. This requires great stillness and non-activity on a regular basis.

Currently, our culture doesn't accept or support this concept of apparent non-activity producing good for all. I see it as our loss, to disconnect ourselves from this human intuitive technology. We support bipolar people who have "made it," i.e., produced something tangible in this reality, which we can all see as good.

We have all witnessed bipolar individuals in their current passion going for it. Productivity, charisma, and excellence in customer service are evident in these times. This could be a job they love serving people, selling something, fixing, or creating. Are we able to accept that these times of super functioning may come from times of stillness when business is slower and super function mode is not currently needed?

I agree, authenticity in this endeavor is an ongoing challenge. How balanced is the individual? How much are willing to support them in finding balance? Are they currently heading in a positive direction or self-destruct? Is it worth the benefit of their super function times, to support them when they are not?

This is why we don't always support bipolar individuals in struggling to understand and seek their truth, which is vital for their balanced existence. This is where the bipolar experience is a tragedy and a missed opportunity by all. Trust as a culture that we may not know all and see all yet and that our future bipolar children and present bipolar members of our tribe are worthy of trust. This is a gift we need to give ourselves in order to redeem the full benefit of the bipolar opportunity.

Epilogue

There was a time ...

There was a time when darkness ruled my life. Internal hell was my mode, and I was continually reinventing insanity around me so that I could retreat further into my shelter space, deep inside. I was a master of the art form of being invisible and miserable in a crowd full of happy people. I was in constant motion throughout my day with jobs, people, friends, and living spaces. I had become the darkness learned long ago, and I perpetuated beliefs around me to avoid the pain of dealing with it. It was a prison. I was aware of the prison I was in, and could see the claw marks on my inner walls; I was craving to get out and was jumping up to grab the bars and briefly smile at people before my strength to be happy gave out, and then I would collapse onto the cold stone floor of my cell, surrendering again to the darkness, comforting myself with thoughts of suicide.

Now is a time ...

Life is good, life is up, life is down, and life is okay. I am a healer. I am a voice. I am a learner. My past is a dusty book on the shelf which I've mostly forgotten about. Internal hell is not my norm; internal ocean, in dance with my tribe, is becoming my norm. Some days are dark and stormy, but most days are calm and somewhat still. My cold stone cell inside now has open windows, and the carvings of this book, I've etched on the walls in desperation over twenty years, to free myself. On days when I visit my cell, I use them to free myself again from the darkness still evaporating from my belief in lack. Suicide is an old and familiar friend I'm no longer scared of. I welcome him in and enjoy a cup of tea and stillness. We talk, he is very wise, and he sees beyond limitations I accept when I'm comfortable in normal. He threatens my world from time to time, yet has become more of a guide for seeing the false truths I attempt to live when avoiding my true passions.

Our Journey began … ***at a campfire, long ago.***

… … …

It's a clear night, and the stars are out. Sparks drift up from the spruce wood flames. A dark ring is forming around the base of the fire as the snow melts. We are bundled up in bearskins; our tummies are full because the hunters were skillful today. An old woman comes to the fire; it's immediately silent and still. A quiet shiver winds its way up everyone's spine, no one is immune to her immense, silent power. She is our guide in the unknown. She knows the ways of healing. I'm a little child near her feet, scared because I know tomorrow my training with her starts. I don't know why, but the elders have chosen me to be a healer and not a hunter. I don't like hunting anyway, but the healer seems crazy to me. But people think I'm crazy too.
I watch her grey hair sway as she finds a way to her seat by the fire. No one says a word until she grunts, indicating tonight is not a night for words from her. The hunters pick up their tale again from the day's adventures, and I hold my mom tight, because tomorrow I go far away to the caves with the other special children, led by the crazy woman …

Three months later after initial training … or slowly digesting this book …

My nostrils taste the spruce smoke before we see the glare; a few sparks emerge above the trees surrounding the elders' council. I am back from the caves with the crazy woman. Tonight, I meet my mentor. He's not a traditional healer in any way, like she is. He doesn't have many holdings. He just is. It's been said he's been to the far unknown lands and beyond. Some say he'll go weeks without a spoken word or stay in his shack away from the others for days at a time, muttering. The elders say he is the keeper of the mystery. They say he is driven with the questions none of us think about, yet ask when we are alone, or near death. He speaks at council in times of strife. He is our guide in the quiet. No one knows him, but he knows us all. He is the keeper of hope. They called me happy/sad boy, moody/silent child. They don't know what else to do with me, so they'll give me to the keeper of mysteries. He's getting on in years, they hope I'll somehow figure out what he does ... as I get closer to the fire, his eyes penetrate my soul.